*Never Too Late
to
Internet Date*

Never Too Late to Internet Date

a guide to finding new relationships

by Carol Thomas

Westcom Press
Culver City, California

Copyright © 2018 by Carol Thomas
CarolThomas2239@gmail.com

Printed in the United States of America

All rights reserved. No part of this publication may be reproduced, stored in any retrieval system, or transmitted in any form or by any means, mechanical, photocopying, recording or otherwise, without permission in writing from the publisher, except by a reviewer, who may quote brief passages in a review.

Published by:
Westcom Press, LLC
10736 Jefferson Boulevard, Suite 383
Culver City, CA 90230
westcom.press@mac.com

ISBN: 978-1-938620-23-2

Library of Congress Control Number: 2018948420

Retail Price: US$12.95

Acknowledgements

I thank my many friends who generously shared their stories of internet dating. Your laughter, guidance, and experiences helped fill the pages of this book.

I also thank each new man I dated; you, too, contributed a page or two or three to my book. You also gave me hope that along this path I will find a new love.

Table of Contents

Acknowledgements v
Introduction ix
Chapter 1. Are You Ready to Date? 1
Chapter 2. Popular Dating Sites 15
Chapter 3. Writing Your Profile 23
Chapter 4. Your New Self-Image 37
Chapter 5. Modern Dating Do's and Don'ts 49
Chapter 6. Getting Ready for the Bedroom 67
Chapter 7. Sex and Sleepovers 81
Chapter 8. An Affair (Not) to Remember 89
Chapter 9. The Cowboy 103
Chapter 10. Boys and Their Toys,
and the Games They Play 115
Chapter 11. It's Not All About *You* 123
Conclusion 127
Appendix: Stay Healthy and Safe 131
About the Author 137
Dedication 139

Introduction

The purpose of our lives is to be happy.
—**Dalai Lama**

When we were young, senior life seemed a hundred years away. Suddenly without warning, it's here.

What if it's not the life we always imagined?

If you'd told me a few years ago that I'd publish an advice book for seniors based on my internet dating experiences, I would have laughed, *"Impossible!"*

Well, the impossible happens when we least expect it. After fifty wonderful years, my married life ended with a doctor's devastating diagnosis. Becoming a widow was not an option I'd ever imagined; my husband had always been healthy and vibrant, and I'd thought I'd always be part of a couple. Now I was forced to realize I might be alone for the rest of my life.

I was lucky to have children and friends who were there for me, but I still had days and nights of loneliness, anger, and sadness. Finally, after two long years and many tears, I knew it was time to be happy again; I was ready for companionship, romance, perhaps even another love. But where to begin?

My dating skills were rusty—it'd been well over fifty years since my last blind date. I wasn't sure how to put myself out there, and I didn't know any single, age-appropriate men. Would a charming gentleman want to hold my hand, dance with me in the kitchen, and take me to bed? Would I want to go?

I asked family and friends for advice, and reviews were mixed. Some were skeptical and some were happy that I was ready to look for someone new in my life. This put the decision right back where it belonged—on me. I knew it was time to become responsible for my own future, and I couldn't expect friends or family members to find someone for me.

I did what any of us should do when we start a brand-new project—I researched the best way to move forward and find eligible men. This turned

Introduction

out to be the easy part: Internet dating was the best and safest route for me, everyone agreed.

> *Only I can change my life. No one can do it for me.*
> —**Carol Burnett**

Then I continued my research at my local Barnes & Noble store. When I navigated the self-help section for the first time in my life, I was disappointed to discover most dating books were written by men. I scanned the shelves and couldn't find the book I needed, a book written *by* a women *for* a woman like me.

As I stood in the middle of Barnes & Noble, I promised myself, "If I survive this adventure, no matter *how* it turns out, I'll write a book to encourage and advise others about the tricky subject of dating senior-style."

Tricky is right! Dating has changed over the last fifty years, not even counting computers and the online element. How could I get into the dating game, have fun, and keep my dignity? Then I laughed at myself. How important *was* dignity in the scheme of things?

Once I began exploring the world of internet dating, I learned that roles have switched around in ways I'd never imagined. If you've been married for a majority of your entire adult life, you're probably unaware of all the modern ins and outs of dating.

Yes, friends, you will have many new experiences and find many new roles to play.

Happily, any stigma associated with women and men over sixty dating has vanished. *Seniors meet, date, and sleep with each other far more often than you might think.*

The fact that you are actively looking for a partner on the internet is not a crime, but an adventure.

My book will reassure you that you aren't alone, and it will help you navigate through this brave new world of internet dating.

Many men and women share their dating experiences in my book, and I hope you'll enjoy their adventures and laugh along with us. In my wildest dreams, I can barely imagine having as much fun as they've had as they travel down the internet highway. Of course, I use pseudonyms throughout the book, and all names have been changed to protect the innocent (and the guilty!).

When you spread the word to your friends that you're searching online, no doubt you'll hear, "About time! Me too." Many people say they've met their Mr. Right through a friend, but nine times out of ten, that "friend" is an internet dating site.

Never Too Late To Internet Date is straightforward and painfully honest, and we'll explore many subjects, from setting up your online profile,

Introduction

to your first date, and even sex and sleepovers. I hope my candor will help you reflect on yourself, how you see others, and how you want others to see you.

I've learned I can be happy again, and I *know* you want to be happy or you wouldn't have chosen to pick up this book. There will be ups and downs on your dating journey, and many surprises await you. It takes courage, wisdom, and all the life experiences you can muster.

As Lucille Ball said, *"I believe that we're as happy in life as we make up our minds to be."*

Make up *your* mind to be happy, and let your adventure begin.

1

Are You Ready to Date?

The only failure is not to try.
—George Clooney

Do you sit at home alone every night watching television or reading a book? Are you tired of making excuses when you call an old friend to just to hear a friendly voice? Do you miss intimacy?

I have the solution for you, and it's not something we could have possibly imagined when we were young.

It's the brave new world of internet dating!

Though the rules and practices have changed from the last time you were in the dating game, they are remarkably easy to learn. Your rewards are companionship, fun, romance, and (if you want it!) maybe even sex.

I'm here to help you avoid the rough patches as you get back into the swing of dating.

It's a difficult spot to be in when life plays a cruel trick on you and you are the one left from a relationship you thought would last forever. Making the decision to start dating again is a truly tough one. It means you're moving on, which is not easy.

You will need a period of adjustment. Don't let people push you into it; take your time, but don't isolate yourself *too* long.

During our married life, my husband and I always socialized with other married couples. I've heard from many other widows how lucky I was that our friends continued to include me in their activities after my husband died. Friends from my marriage were my lifesavers during my adjustment period. Still, as time passed during those few years, I began to feel a bit like a fifth wheel. If you've always been part of a couple, being the only single in the group can be less comfortable than you'd imagined.

Once you're ready, once you've honestly made the decision and you can stand in front of the mirror, look yourself in the eye, and say, *"I am ready to begin finding someone new,"* your life will have fresh meaning and new direction.

You can say with a smile, *"Today is the start of*

the rest of my life." You'll have another reason to check your computer or phone to see if "you've got mail." It's a game that single adults play every day, and it can be very rewarding.

Believe me, you will be *amazed* how exciting this game can be.

I cautioned myself that dating at my age might be a bit awkward. Well, that was an understatement! **Boyfriends are not husbands**; it takes a while to feel at ease with someone new. Your first date will not be as comfortable as your 12,000th evening at home with your husband.

You may even have the urge to hide in the closet the first time you take your clothes off in front of a new man. That's all right. You'll survive, and most likely you will thrive.

The brave new world

There were no dating candidates among the people I knew, so my only alternative was looking outside my known acquaintances. That meant meeting strangers, which I found a bit intimidating. After considering my options, I still felt the best and safest choice was internet dating.

You join a dating site looking for companionship, love, and perhaps someone to be your life partner. If you are lucky enough to pop up in each other's daily matches, you may find your next love.

Yes, some men and women criticize the concept of online dating, and a few say that using a dating site is a last resort, but millions of users disagree. I do, too!

The internet introduces you to a variety of people you might never meet otherwise—some most certainly will take you out of your comfort zone. In any case, these new people will all add to your life experience, and perhaps give you a new view or change a long-held opinion.

> *Seize the moment of happiness, love and be loved. That is the only reality in the world; all else is folly.*
>
> **—Leo Tolstoy**

If you are intimidated by a smart phone or a computer, internet dating will give you the purpose for learning new skills. Though my technical skills were never my strong suit, I knew enough to cope. I know how to use my cell phone for texting as well as calling, and I have basic computer and internet skills, although I am by no means a computer expert and sometimes struggle. Still, I figured I've managed to handle the technological changes that life has thrown at me for seventy years, so I could handle this challenge, too. I only needed help to set up my profile, which I'll explain in the next chapter.

Are You Ready to Date?

There were *so* many sites to choose from. After quite a bit of research and internet searching, I chose a site that seemed compatible and dove right in. Getting set up took more time than I expected, and I needed more help than I planned. Still, before I could change my mind, I was out there surfing on the World Wide Web.

Surfing online in my home office gave me the privacy to review the profiles I saw and decide what I liked and didn't like about the men I was viewing. It was amazingly comfortable to sit hidden from the world, reading the thoughts, histories, and desires of men.

Searching on your dating site is like shopping; you go to the appropriate internet store, browse through the departments, pick a face off the rack, make contact, and sometimes try them on. Some fit and others you put back on the rack.

My nights were spent screening the profiles of men I could only imagine meeting. When I first began, I was skeptical, but it wasn't long before I wondered if my profile would interest the men I was viewing. I realized all of us involved in this process are creating our online ads, and I felt like I almost needed to hire a marketing manager to get the right man. To put it simply and honestly, we're advertising ourselves.

When you first join a dating site, you are the new kid on the block, and you'll receive a barrage of emails from a wide variety of men. Regulars on the internet are quick to recognize a new face. It was flattering at first, then it was obvious many of these men didn't appeal to me. I gave every man who responded to my profile the courtesy of a quick, polite thank you even if I had no intention of dating him.

Don't expect the same courtesy in return. Most men don't bother to acknowledge a woman if they don't intend to date her. I still find it frustrating when a man isn't courteous to a woman who's taken her time to write him.

Lack of response is the number one complaint I hear from women everywhere. As a test, I wrote to ten wildly different men, all of whom I thought were good matches. I received *one* response. Was I miffed? You bet. I had taken my time to write something very nice to each of them, and nine of them didn't even acknowledge receipt of my note.

My internet dating website tells me, for a nominal fee, when a man reads my notes. Guess what? All ten notes were received and read. I mused, "What has happened to modern manners?"

Finally, I had to come to grips with the fact that that

Are You Ready to Date?

I'm not the only one who's not being acknowledged. This is the new reality; this is how we live now, without thank-you notes and acknowledgments. You must gracefully accept that most men handle internet dating communications this way.

Given the ratio of women to men, it's almost understandable. They have so many choices!

You're not alone

When I broke my silence and finally started to talk to my single friends about internet dating, I was amazed at the dating stories that came pouring out. I had *no* clue that many of these men and women wanted to meet someone new, much less on internet dating sites. They were online in droves.

Everyone is *so* secretive until they know you are one of them. Then, suddenly, friends are checking in with you, and you're having fun together as you share stories and laugh. Many had been through the same situations I was experiencing, and they shared some very important tips I hadn't figured out for myself.

The most important modern fact I learned was counterintuitive to me: *Women must usually reach out to the men*. Women need to instigate the conversation rather than wait for men to contact us. This isn't natural for me, or for many women for that matter, and it can put us out of our comfort zone.

My more experienced friends also explained that men will often exchange a few emails, make a call, sound really interested, promise to call again for a date, and then vanish without a trace. It was hard to understand, but finally I accepted that sometimes grown men act like little boys.

I also learned that women shouldn't play coy games, either.

When someone reaches out to contact you, don't play hard-to-get and wait two days to respond. Take a minute *now* and write a quick email, *especially* if you are interested. Even if you're not, I hope you will still send an email to thank him for contacting you. It doesn't take much time to write, "Sorry, but we are not a match."

As I became more comfortable with my dating situation and began to have more email interactions with men, I moved quickly to having telephone conversation with men I liked. I was glad to learn it's common to exchange phone numbers once you feel comfortable with your connection. To me, there's no substitute for the human voice, and I felt it was important to talk with a man before our first date.

Are You Ready to Date?

A person may not write well or be able to express himself with written words on a computer but may communicate well on a phone. A friendly, warm voice can break down barriers. It's easy to ask questions and learn more about him and it gives you an opportunity to ask for a last name so you can Google them. I can talk and Google at the same time. Can you?

Speaking with someone can be a turn-on or a turn-off. My standards are particularly high, I admit, when it comes to spoken communications: If I don't care for the voice on the other end of the conversation or feel we didn't make a connection on the phone, the man never makes it to a first date. It's a good screening process for me and many of my friends. Another good test is to imagine that voice beside you on the pillow. I close my eyes, and, if his voice sounds pleasing, it's a plus.

Be honest with yourself in the new, modern dating world. Realize that once a positive connection is made, sex is on the table. Sex seems to be the number one thing on men's minds these days. Maybe it always was, but I was too married to notice. Be prepared, because men will ask you on the first date if you are still interested in sexual relations.

Relax, it doesn't mean you're committed to

sleep with them. It just means you'll consider it. Sure, there are some men who just want companionship or platonic intimacy, but they are few and far between.

One of my favorite dates was a retired television and movie actor who was ten years older than he looked in the professionally-taken photos on his profile. Of course, I recognized his face from the daytime television shows and movies he had appeared in years before. He had been very successful all his life, and though he now was in a wheelchair, his zest for life was unmistakable. Since he was determined to continue going out with lovely ladies as he had done throughout his professional career, he used the dating site to find them and a chauffeur to keep him mobile.

He was handsome and very eloquent; twenty years earlier, he would have been a great catch (or match!) for any woman. His reason for dating was to keep himself young. He wasn't looking for sex, romantic love, or even a long-term relationship, just companionship—with a rotating cast of different women. It was fun to be one of them for an all-too-brief time. I felt like the star of my own soap opera.

My one and only celebrity date never made it to the casting couch.

Are You Ready to Date?

Making choices

Be honest with yourself when you choose the parameters for your dates. If you are choosing only the handsome gentlemen in suits and ties, take a moment to imagine whom you might be missing. The men you skip over may be strong, worldly, and wise—or affectionate and sexy!—and looking for a nice woman to love and spoil. Be open-minded and give them a chance. You may be surprised.

Many of us would like Mr. Tall, Dark and Handsome, but the type is few and far between on any dating site I have viewed. The few who go on dating sites are snatched up quickly, and their life cycle on the site can be measured in hours and days, not weeks and months.

Be forgiving of typos. If a man says he is three feet, four inches tall, he probably touched the wrong key on his computer, and, believe it or not, he may be six feet, four inches. When I first started dating and saw such obvious errors, I innocently asked about them. I was quickly reminded that most men don't like to be caught in an error—or, even worse, be corrected.

Now I'm wiser, and when I see an obviously incorrect fact or possible typo, I just ignore it. Trust me, I see such mistakes often.

Never Too Late to Internet Date

For the first three months I focused solely on widowers. I'd been married a long time, and I was sure we would have more in common and I would relate better to them. My thoughts were simple: *Do we have similar interests? Will I want to kiss him? Will he like my cooking? Does he dress well? Will my children like him? Might we make a good couple??* If we didn't fit, I quickly clicked on the next face.

I live in the Palm Springs area where many men are looking for a lady golfer. I don't golf, but I do own a golf cart. When first I wrote to golfers online, I happily offered to drive them around the course or fix them dinner after their rounds. That got me nowhere.

I learned that single golfers play their eighteen holes with their buddies (not alone with a non-golfer), go back to the club house to have a drink or two with the boys, have dinner, discuss their scores, and spend time exchanging golf stories, which usually consist of why they missed that six-foot putt on the third hole.

Though my husband was an avid golfer, he always came home for dinner. Now that I am single and can understand the plight of the single golfer, I have come to accept that the post-golf ritual is unshakable. You're not going to be a part of it unless you are a golfer yourself and can play a round with him and his two closest buddies.

Some people just want a partner who is good company, someone to spend time with them. I'm looking for a more intimate version of that relationship, with romance and adventure mixed in.

And some men and women *are* looking for the ring and happily ever after. While remarriage rates are higher than ever for those of us over 60, there are some caveats you need to know if you're looking to tie the knot with someone new.

I strongly advise you against seriously dating a recently divorced or separated person. While you may want to help him (or her) heal, their emotional baggage will become part of your relationship, and you have no idea just how seriously their family problems or personal trauma may affect them. Your good intentions won't stop anyone from possibly leaving you behind after you helped them adjust to single life.

Widows and widowers have their own unique baggage. While those who had happy marriages *are* more likely to remarry, some men and women can never get over the loss of their beloved spouse. You can't change that no matter how hard you try. A very strong ongoing connection to a previous partner should send up a serious red flag.

Never Too Late to Internet Date

A wonderful gentleman confessed to me that after his wife of forty years passed away, he could no longer sleep in their bed. Her clothes were still hanging in the closet three years after her death. He thought he was ready to move into the dating world, but he wasn't. Someone still so attached may think he is looking for a new partner, but he is not ready for another serious relationship.

This applies to you, too. Take a good look around your own emotional baggage. I was surprised when a very good friend suggested I move the many photos of my husband from the living room to another part of the house. I was hesitant, but she was right. Photos bring back many wonderful memories, but if you are truly trying to start a new life, put the pictures into a photo album or hang them in your own private space.

When you start dating, your life will grow and change. Your friends and family may think you're a bit daffy. You will change your mind many times during the dating process, but don't forget this: The more men you meet, the easier the decision will be when you finally find your new love—The One!

Remind yourself that happiness is a *choice*, not a destination.

2

Popular Dating Sites

> *Love is like a virus.*
> *It can happen to anyone at any time.*
> —**Maya Angelou**

*Y*ou'll find many dating sites to select from, and they're all slightly different. Each site has a focus on specific age brackets, ethnic groups, religions, or expectations. Once you sign up for the first site, ads for more pop up on the top of your screen every day, enticing you to join and spend your hard-earned retirement money. Some are free (at least for basic services), and some charge thousands of dollars. Choose wisely!

Never Too Late to Internet Date

<u>Here are a few of the top dating sites:</u>

Zoosk.com, 4 stars, 9.8 rating. Only if you have solid tech skills.

Match.com, 5 stars, 9.3 rating. Age 25 to 50 plus.

eHarmony.com, 4 stars, 8.8 rating. For those looking for long-term relationship or perhaps marriage.

OurTime.com, 4 stars, 8.6 rating. For mature singles, 50+ only.

SinglePeopleMeet.com, 8.3 rating. May be the best site for seniors wanting love.

PlentyofFish.com, (aka "POF"), 4 stars, 8.5 rating. A free site, for ages 18 to 55 plus.

AARP Dating Service, Available to AARP members only.

JDate.com, For Jewish singles.

EliteSingles.com, 5 star, 9.7 rating, for educated professionals age 25 to 49.

ChristianCafé.com, For every denomination of Christian.

Mingle2.com, A free site for all ages.

Silver Singles, 8.4 rating.

Popular Dating Sites

You may want to be wary of *It's Just Lunch*, a site you've probably seen advertised quite a bit—that's a site for the working fifty-something crowd. When I joined this website, I quickly learned it was not for me. Once I saw all the handsome young forty- and fifty-year-old men, I canceled the next morning, and my membership money was quickly refunded.

Sites will be cooperative if you decide to cancel—*if* you call promptly. If you use the services for twenty-nine days and then call to cancel, don't expect the same courtesy.

> *All your dreams come true if you have the courage to pursue them.*
> —**Walt Disney**

It pays to investigate all the sites before you spend your money. Study all the options any site offers. Watch carefully, as some sites charge for extras services such as being notified when someone has viewed your profile or being able to see how long a prospect spends online. The extras are optional, and sometimes they're worth it.

Sites will encourage you to renew your membership; be aware that most dating sites will renew automatically. You must check the "do not renew" box on your sign-up settings to avoid auto-charges; once they have access to your card number, it's buyer beware. I suggest you make sure to monitor your credit card statement.

Even some of the "free" sites charge you money in return for access to more information about your prospective date. If you want these extra facts, consider investing in their premium services for a few dollars per month.

One of the largest free dating sites is *Plenty of Fish*, which has a very catchy title. I laugh when I think that if you catch a fish and don't like their size or shape, you just throw them back into the pond for someone else to hook. The internet gives us a large sea to fish in. I have many friends who use this free dating site exclusively, and they have hooked some good catches. A friend recently married the "fish" she caught.

Some sites specialize in sex with no strings attached; a few are HookUp.com, EasySex.com, OKCupid.com. If you are looking for a one-night stand and not a real relationship, they will fill your needs.

I am on more than one site, as are most of the people I meet. While sites do specialize, there's quite a bit of overlap. Because of my research, I have seen many of the same faces on two or three sites.

How much you spend on dating sites is up to you and your bank account. Many people join exclusive, high-end dating sites and pay up to ten

Popular Dating Sites

thousand dollars for memberships guaranteeing them a perfect mate. Photos, CDs and other special bonuses are included, of course. If that's your cup of tea, and you can afford the price, give it a try. Millionaire.com might be the site for you.

Bumble is a popular app for your phone that's free and easy to set up; the only prerequisite is that you must be on Facebook. It's a little different to use, and to be successful you should be comfortable with your smartphone. There are many seniors using the app, and it's a good alternative to the usual sites.

A seventy-eight-year old friend of mine joined a fifty-something dating site by accident, paying six months in advance. Of course, she never made a real connection on the site. Instead, many men had the gall to send her requests for money, assuming she was well-off and looking to enjoy the company of younger men, for a price.

Please be aware: Once you're online and have registered at one or more sites, you may be approached by men who will ask you for money at some point in a relationship. Scammers are a big issue throughout the internet, on social media and email as well as dating sites. Some of the hard-luck stories are quite believable; they range from stranded tourists to family and health crises.

Never Too Late to Internet Date

Never, never disclose your financial information. This is the reason I strongly advise you to avoid including any details about income on your profile. It's the one place on your dating website questionnaire where "I will tell you later" may apply.

Your best protection is to learn how to screen the inquiries and replies you receive, and practice safe connections. As careful as you might be, some scammers will still approach you. Please report them to the dating site without hesitation.

When I was contacted by a man from Texas, I politely wrote back that we lived miles apart but thanked him for his interest. He responded disarmingly that he worked in the Los Angeles area, had his own private plane, and would fly to the Los Angeles area to meet me. We emailed back and forth a few times before he asked for my phone number. Standard dating procedure, right?

When he called me, within five minutes he asked who did my financial planning. I tried to change the subject twice, saying my investments were in place, but he continued asking about my lifestyle in a very personal manner. He excused his probing by saying that he liked having background on the women he dated.

A red flag went up; I consider myself a savvy

Popular Dating Sites

senior. I pretended that my phone had a bad connection, got off the line, and turned him in to my dating site as a possible scammer. He's never called back. I hope you would have done the same, experienced dater or not.

3

Writing Your Profile

*Just remember, you are absolutely unique
—just like everyone else.*
—**Andy Warhol**

Your profile is your billboard in the world of internet dating, and it's the single most important part of the process. You're giving your prospective date a first glimpse into your life, and that peek needs to be interesting, exciting, honest, and as clever as you can make it. Remember, everyone in the dating world is peering into their computer, searching for the right mate.

The fast-paced world we seniors live in is full of tech-savvy people, and you will need to be somewhat competent with your computer, phone, or tablet. If you're not computer-literate, you'll be at a severe disadvantage in the world of internet dating.

If you know your technical skills need some help, a computer class will get you up to speed. Learning is good for brains of any age. Also, the new skills you master will help make your venture into online dating easier, more fun, and a lot more stress-free.

Fortunately, classes are available everywhere. In addition to free classes offered by your tablet or phone supplier, check the class schedules at your local community college, library, or senior center. Check the newspaper for times and places, and don't be shy. If you know how to access the internet, Google for tutorials on YouTube.

I recently attended iPad classes at my local library. My mentor-teacher was a fourteen-year-old high school student who was not only smart and up to date on all the latest gadgets, but she was a great instructor. Register and attend some classes; who knows, you might meet someone who will ask you out for coffee, just like in high school.

This is a good time to introduce your children and family to the idea of your internet dating life. Ask them for some help with the technical part of setting up your profile.

Dating sites explain the process if you carefully

Writing Your Profile

read and follow all the instructions on their profile page. There is always a list of questions and instructions, usually on the left side of the screen; make sure you take time to read through the entire list, since all sites are different.

When you write your user profile, maintain a warm, friendly, honest tone throughout the process. Don't be afraid to brag a bit, but always be truthful. Your profile sets the tone of any future relationship; it gives your prospective date your basic information, and it also reveals an outline of the person you are interested in meeting.

The first step is to select your user name, which is one of the most important decisions you make. It's also the *one* item your dating site will not allow you to change or edit later. Be cautious and give it some thought. Make sure your user name is memorable as well as clever, and a name you're comfortable being called.

When I set up my profile with my oldest daughter's help, she chose my user name and I am still reeling from the choice I agreed to—a youthful, beachy-sounding name. She thought my love of the beach should dictate my name, and though *I* think I'm too old for the name, I smile when I think of how she sees me. Sitting with her and laughing as we wrote my profile was one of the best mother-daughter moments *ever*, and I highly recommend the experience. Still, I'm forever stuck with the name we chose for my favorite dating site

As part of your profile, you'll also need to supply your birth date and year, height, eye color, ethnicity, profession; also your drinking and smoking habits, your body type, and whether you're divorced, widowed, or separated.

One of the most important questions you need to answer honestly is the type of relationship you want. Do you want to simply date for fun, do you want a long-term relationship, or are you looking for someone to marry? Some sites offer the option of "activity partner." What type of "activity" they mean is anyone's guess.

I recommend you avoid including your yearly income within your profile. Many seniors live on their social security and a pension, but there are also some in the six-digit bracket. Granted, you may be much more sought-after in the higher income brackets, but that's not necessarily the best reason to be desired. *It's your responsibility to be diligent and protect your personal information.*

Photos are the first thing a prospective date sees, often the only thing. You need to post a current, flattering picture that looks like *you*. Consider your photo as your advertisement.

Writing Your Profile

My honest profile has always brought praise from gentlemen I met. I don't lie about my age, height, or weight, and I always hear, "You look just like your picture." It's a welcome compliment. When you connect with a new man, he should be able to recognize you as you enter the room.

This is a good time to decide if you are going to update your hairstyle, perhaps even its color. Make the decision before you spend money and time on a profile photo.

Be true to yourself! Many dating friends say that most men and women they meet on dating sites are much older in person than their photos; of course, this means they lied about their age. Men tell me they've met women who posted photos of their daughters and claim the pictures as their own. Give me a *break*, ladies! Remember, you want to meet that man in person someday. What will he think of you *then*?

Check out the services of a photographer. I invested in a professional profile shot and justified the expense by giving framed copies to my family members for Christmas. Another option, of course, is to ask a talented friend to take photos of you on a cell phone. Take dozens of pictures and don't hesitate to use the delete feature.

I've seen too many profile pictures of men

with a tell-tale shower curtain hanging behind as a backdrop. If all you can come up with is a selfie taken in your bathroom mirror, you need help. Call your grandchildren or a friend who can make sure you present yourself attractively.

The worst profile shot I've seen was a selfie of a man sitting on the toilet with his arm outstretched. The funny thing was he got the entire scene, not just his face. He must not have checked the photo before posting it to his dating site. I hate to think he did it intentionally! How could he think any woman would ever be attracted to him after seeing that shot?

Your profile setup allows body type options, and many people choose "a few extra pounds." I have a friend who calls that the five-thirty rule—people lie about their age by five or even ten years and their weight by thirty pounds. You will barely recognize them if you finally get together for that first date.

All profiles ask you to list your personal interests. Don't just check one or two things you're doing now. Check everything you would be doing if your single status didn't cramp your style plus all the things you'd like to learn. If you've always wanted to attend more theaters and museums or take computer classes, check the boxes. Do you want to hike? Check! Go to vineyards and wine tastings? Check!

Writing Your Profile

Take salsa lessons? Check! You might find someone who also wants to do those things and would love to do them on your first date.

> *Anyone who stops learning is old, whether at 20 or 80. Anyone who keeps learning stays young. The greatest thing in life is to keep your mind young.*
>
> **—Henry Ford**

The number one thing to check is *coffee and conversation*, because that's a popular, relaxed way to have a first meeting. There's a Starbucks on every corner, and it's a safe place to meet. If you don't like Starbucks, list your favorite gourmet coffee or tea shop, café, or casual neighborhood hang-out.

Alumni connections are useful for identifying potential matches and finding old friends. You'd be surprised how often high school friends meet again through the internet and date after decades without contact.

Other popular activities are fishing, hunting, politics, hobbies and crafts, exploring new areas, swimming, and volunteering. Men love a woman who likes to cook, travel, and watch sports.

When I view a new match and the man has checked off all the categories designated by the dating site but didn't write a single line about himself in the *in my own words* section, I assume he's afraid to put himself out there, or he may not have good computer skills.

I won't respond to a man who doesn't post a photo. On my own profile, I clearly warn all prospective dates: "No photo, no reply." You'll be surprised how many men don't seem to read a woman's entire profile. They only look at the picture.

When you're scanning profiles, it's very annoying to see someone avoid an answer and check "I will tell you later." Everyone wants to know *now*. I can guarantee that your prospective date won't return to your profile later to see if you have finished your computer résumé or bother to set up a date to find out in person.

Dating sites offer long personality tests, so take the time and complete all questions. The tests ask a surprising number of personal questions, and they give you plenty of options. Don't stress over the tests. Remember—the goal is to connect you to someone compatible.

Driving long distances can be a serious issue for seniors, especially at night or in bad weather. When a prospective date is from a city you don't know, take the time to research the location with a Google search before you respond. If it's too far for you to drive, consider that the person you are writing may have the same issue.

Writing Your Profile

If you live in a small town and only want someone nearby, think twice about sticking to your zip code, because choices may be limited. You may want to expand your acceptable radius.

You'll need to choose a radius of miles that's geographically acceptable. Are you looking for a person within twenty-five, fifty, one hundred, or five hundred miles from your zip code? Your choice can eliminate the complication of long-distance relationships. A good rule of thumb is my patented one-hour limit.

Though you may select a small radius when you set up your dating parameters, the site will automatically expand the distance when there aren't enough matches for you to view on any given day. All sites want you to see as many faces as possible. The dating site looks more successful when they show you extra member profiles, even if they aren't in your chosen zip code.

You may see a very appealing face and be intrigued by his profile, but if he lives an hour or two down a busy freeway, getting together may be too difficult for either of you. Unless you're lucky enough to have no driving issues, distance and tricky traffic will cut down your pool of prospective profiles.

I have corresponded with men miles away from

my zip code who were interesting and could have been a perfect match, but, when push comes to shove, we all want someone close to home. He may be the most appealing person in your match selections today, but there will be new faces tomorrow.

(A word of warning: If you do invite an out-of-town gentleman for dinner at your home, he may expect to stay, so get the spare bedroom ready or be prepared to possibly share your bed.)

Retirees are often snowbirds, and it's common for seniors to live and date in two different locations. If someone contacts you from out of state and he piques your interest, be adventurous and respond. Investigate every prospective match as an exciting prospect. You never know where love exists, across the country or just around the corner.

Be stingy with travel photos. Most people believe travel pictures are posted just to impress others. Yes, they show the glamorous places you have visited, but the past is not what you want to emphasize now. If the trip you share was twenty years ago, how does it help show the real you *today*? Many of us have traveled in the past, but our current life is what dating's all about.

What about pictures of your pets? I love dogs and cats as much as the next person, but I'm not going to a dating site to see a parade of animals. A dog

Writing Your Profile

curled up on the sofa or a cat on the kitchen counter is not what I pay my monthly dating site fees to view. Too many times, the dog or cat are pictured by themselves. There's not much point to the photos, other than showing someone's softer side.

We all love our grandchildren, but sixteen pictures of family members aren't what people spend money to view. A few are great, but too many family photos can make a prospective date lose interest in a hurry. Men and women are looking for each other, not grandchildren. They are interested in meeting *you*.

Create a positive ending for your profile. This is the time to toot your own horn a bit, and clearly state what you're looking for in a date or partner. My summary reads: "I know somewhere out there is a man who wants an intelligent, romantic, and caring woman. I am active, attractive and available. My photos are current, and I hope yours are too. I have a very positive attitude about life and take pride in myself and my appearance. I consider myself a fun-loving, classy lady. Hope to hear from you soon."

It's incredibly important that you use positive terms when you describe yourself and what you're looking for.

Don't hesitate to be specific and set boundaries;

spelling out your expectations does not make you a date snob. I set high standards for the type of man I am searching for, and you should do the same. My words tell men who I am and show my character. When I get a reply, I know I have truly separated the men from the boys.

If you have been online for a few months and you aren't getting much feedback, evaluate your profile; it's time to make changes. Ask an outspoken, honest male friend to read it, and listen to his feedback. Up your game, change your photos, and make yourself sound more interesting and available. Most bios sound alike, so you must add a spark to make yourself stand out from the crowd.

Your dating site will update your profile and it will post that you have made changes and updated some information. You might get a second look from Mr. Wonderful.

This advice may seem obvious, but the ill-written, misspelled profiles I've seen online imply otherwise:

Read and reread your written profile before you post it—then read it again!

Check for typing errors, and make sure you complete all sentences. Whether you or a friend writes the profile, proofread your copy, and then

Writing Your Profile

read it again, slowly and carefully. You don't have to be a computer whiz to use the spellcheck feature; it really can help. Ask a friend or your favorite grandchild to help you if you're not sure how to use it.

4

Your New Self-Image

> *Beauty begins the moment you decide*
> *to be yourself.*
> —**Coco Chanel**

You've selected your dating site, paid for your subscription, written your profile, posted your photos, and now you're ready to begin your internet dating career. It's *almost* time to sit in front of your computer, enter the modern cyber world, and search for Mr. Right.

Before you move forward, it's time to take an honest, personal look at yourself, both fully dressed and under your clothes. You want to be the best you can be when you head out for your first date.

I am a confident woman, and I have always taken pride in my appearance—without apology, I'll say high maintenance has always been a part of my life. This new dating world opened my eyes to a whole new experience, and I'll share it with you now.

Your public self

Look at yourself as others may see you. This is the perfect time to objectively review the body you face in the mirror every morning. Physical attraction *is* important to most women and men, even if they dismiss the idea as "shallow."

You are applying for the job of girlfriend or boyfriend. The old saying, "dress to impress," is still appropriate.

No matter what shape your body is in, you want your first impression to be as good as possible. If you're not super fit and carry some bulges or extra weight, make the most of this first impression with flattering clothing choices.

If you are a bit hippy, make sure your rearview is as flattering as possible. Before you leave the house, check in a mirror. If your arms are flabby, you can wear longer sleeves. You can camouflage all your bulges with properly sized, well-cut clothes. Color and fabric choices help, too.

There are fantastic spandex undergarments these days which are sold everywhere at varying price points. They hold you in a lot more gently

Your New Self-Image

than you'd expect, and they smooth any bulges. These are definitely not old-fashioned girdles. You will be amazed how much better your clothes fit. Shop around, try some on, and buy a larger size than you'd think so you can enjoy your evening.

A wardrobe update is always a good idea, but don't get caught up in fads your granddaughter might wear. Choose age-appropriate clothing—styles that make you feel pretty and that flatter you—not just what's trendy.

Women and men seem to have the notion that casual dress, very acceptable in today's society, can mean shorts, T-shirts and flip-flops. It may be acceptable on a boat at the river or shopping at the hardware store, but not when you're going out to meet someone new and share a meal or a movie. Men have told me they don't care for Birkenstocks, so I suggest you leave those at home.

If you are not sure what to wear, may I suggest a dress rehearsal. I have done this a few times to make sure I look my best for someone new, not overdone or understated. You need to feel comfortable and confident, happy with what you see in the mirror.

While you're trying on that new dress, if you wonder, "How easily will it come off?" Ha! Sex is on your mind. You're more ready for your first date than you realized.

Never Too Late to Internet Date

If you haven't changed your hairstyle for a while, find a good stylist and trust them to update your look. Try a new color and add some highlights—they will brighten your face and your attitude. Stylists can be expensive, but local beauty schools are everywhere, and they offer excellent services that are also affordable. Make sure you do this before you have your profile picture taken.

Don't be surprised if your date has colored his hair, too; these days men are also opting for color to keep themselves looking younger. Why not?

Look objectively at your makeup habits. It may be time for a change. Are you wearing the same lipstick and eye makeup that you did twenty years ago? Have you ignored the age spots that have suddenly started appearing everywhere?

Local department stores give free makeovers as cosmetic promotions. Beauty seminars are also advertised in your local newspaper paper and on TV. You will be amazed at the brand-new glamour secrets you can learn. Watch your newspaper and call for an appointment.

> *You can't keep changing men, so you settle for changing your lipstick.*
> —**Heather Locklear**

I still treasure the advice given to me years ago by one of my oldest friends, a truly beautiful woman, who told me, "Never go out without makeup on."

You never know who you might run into at the grocery store. A dear friend met a delightful man in the produce department of her local supermarket three years ago when they reached for the peaches at the same time; they've been together ever since. So far, my makeup hasn't helped *me* meet a man in the grocery store, but I do feel prettier while I shop!

Beneath the clothes

Although getting naked and going to bed with someone is probably not your first dating priority, it may well happen. The thought of having a stranger see your body after many years with the same partner can bring great anxiety. Who's the last person who saw you naked, other than your doctor?

If it's been awhile, you may wonder how you can face someone new. It's human nature to think, "What will he think of me?" Believe me, he's probably nervous about the same thing. Men have issues with body image, weight gain, and sagging pectoral muscles, too.

If you are interested in pursuing romance, you will need to become comfortable in your body, even when you take your clothes off. Stand naked in front of a mirror and look at yourself, *really* look at yourself from head to toe. You may laugh a bit, but it will be a good laugh. Here you are, possibly a mother and a grandmother, and you have a lifetime of making good use of this body.

Negative little thoughts may run through your mind. *What will he think of me when I take off my bra? Am I too old or too fat to get back in the game?*

Remember that both men and women can get flabby muscles and skin that seems to crinkle everywhere. Breasts don't stay where they were thirty years ago. He is in the same boat and his fears may run along the same lines. Push the negative thoughts back.

What if you've lost all or part of your breasts to cancer, a very common issue today? You need to discuss this issue before you get to the bedroom. How a man handles this situation tells you much about his character. Someone who is worthy of you will cherish you and see your true inner beauty. Remember, *real men don't love the most beautiful girl in the world. They love the girl who makes their world the most beautiful.*

A widowed friend who had been married for a very long time met a wonderful man, and she was extremely nervous about the first time he would see her naked. I shared one of my favorite secrets,

Your New Self-Image

"Always remember, in the dark there is only room for feelings." If you are nervous, turn out the lights, but don't turn off your desire for someone to touch you because you are afraid your body is not beautiful.

> *To love oneself is the beginning of a lifelong romance.*
> **—Oscar Wilde**

While we can't help growing older, we should present the best image possible on the computer screen and on our first date. Competition for that special someone is fierce, and you just might want a second date with that new man you are getting dressed to meet.

When Bette Davis said, "Getting old is not for sissies," she must have imagined today's world of online dating. If you think the lines on your face don't give away your age, you are only kidding yourself. If you have lied about your age or had your photos altered, you are doing a disservice to yourself and anyone truly looking for a compatible partner on the internet. The lines on our faces catch up with all of us. If you want your wrinkles gone, find a doctor, not a photographer.

That's why God invented plastic surgeons.

Today doctors' offices are full of both female and male patients, and there is no need to be embarrassed if you investigate Botox, fillers, and the many options available today. They can be affordable, and it's a great confidence-builder to know you look your best.

> *Wrinkles should merely indicate where smiles have been.*
> —**Mark Twain**

Still, since I became obsessed with writing this book, I scrutinize both sexes as I've never done before. While I stand in line at the local supermarket, I've observed that men don't seem to take care of themselves as well as women do.

Don't fall into that trap. While you're looking for Mr. Right, don't just sit there! Get out of *your* recliner. Take dance, tennis, or golf lessons; be active in your church or synagogue. Volunteer at your local museum, art gallery, or theater group. Find something to do. Try the gym, try anything—just don't sit!

Evaluating men

As we sift through the gentlemen sent to us on our daily matches, we may search just for our perfect Mr. Wonderful. It took me awhile to realize that we tend to overlook the everyday man—the truly genuine and kind man who may not be the best looking, but just might possibly be a gentle and

Your New Self-Image

very caring soul waiting for you to find him.

Looking back on my early online experiences, I realize I did just that. I should have looked beyond the surface of the men I dated. I dismissed far too many men for shallow reasons.

If you like someone you see on a dating site, pay them a compliment in your first email. Some men are starved for compliments, and even handsome men appreciate knowing you find them attractive. It's not necessarily bad to stroke a person's ego.

It's a real treat when a man's photo shows him in a dress shirt or golf attire. Heaven bless the man who dons a sport coat in this modern age of casual dress. They are few and far between on my dating sites, and they make an impact, at least to me.

What if you meet someone and you really like him, but he is a terrible dresser—what should you do? You may have many things in common, travel, theater, cards, but he may look like he never left the fifties. What do you feel comfortable saying?

This can be tricky. It depends how receptive you sense he is to input of this type. If you give feedback, will he be hurt, mad, or grateful because his dear wife always chose his clothes? You better know the answer to that question before you say a word.

Once you're comfortable enough with your relationship to talk about clothing issues, you'll probably know whether he can't afford a better wardrobe or just doesn't care. Some men just *don't* care!

Men's eyebrows usually give away their ages. If the hair on top is brown but the eyebrows are gray, he could be coloring his hair. That doesn't mean he's lying about his age, but he's trying to project a youthful vitality. Covering up wrinkles also might be the reason so many men are sporting a beard or mustache today. If they only realized they're not covering up the lines around their eyes and mouth.

Part of the due diligence I do with dates is finding out where and how they live. I hate to admit it, but our address and the car we drive are reflections on who we are (or want to be). If you are turned on by a BMW convertible, a man with a Chevy truck is possibly not for you, although a Chevy truck can be very exciting if you've never ridden in one.

A man's car says a lot about himself in other ways, too. If he opens the door and the car's a mess, cluttered with fast food wrappers, his home will probably be a mess, too.

You will get a great deal of insight into your dates from how they live. I was invited to a gentleman's home after we had gone out a couple of times, and I was shocked at how he lived. Not only was his house a terrible mess, it was a shrine to his long-departed wife. Seeing that told me he would never move on, so *I* did.

Health issues

A man over 60 is likely to have at least one health issue, and some can directly affect his ego and his sexuality. A man who is truly interested in a woman will be open about his problems, and that says a lot about the faith and confidence he has in you.

Prostate cancer is one of the many diseases that can leave a man unable to perform sexually, a devastating issue for most men. Since I have been on dating sites, I have learned more about the prostate than I care to share with you, from pellet and chemo treatments to their side effects.

Be prepared for a different kind of romance when a man talks about his inability to have sexual relations. Be supportive and compassionate and realize how hard it is for most men to discuss these private matters. This may be awkward at first for a man, but talking about his issues will help you find new ways to please each other and may lead to some wonderful experiences.

My friend Liz is very happy with a man she met online, who was upfront about his inability to have traditional sexual intercourse. He told her, "We may not do what you're used to, but I promise you'll always leave with a smile on your face!" She's still smiling.

When you get to know your special person, confide in each other. Talk about your life and personal issues with the assurance that you want a new beginning and are working hard to achieve that goal.

5

Modern Dating Do's and Don'ts

All progress takes place out of your comfort zone.
—**Michael Bobok**

Senior dating has a learning curve and it requires an entirely new set of skills. Be aware that you bring along a lot of baggage from the last few decades, and so do your dates.

Your first internet date will probably be a nerve-wracking experience wrapped in great anticipation. You are excited, a little scared, and you may have some doubts, especially if it's been decades since you've been on a date with someone new. You can find consolation in knowing that your date may be just as nervous as you. We are all being transported back to the days of our youth, and our youth is *way* behind us.

My feelings were mixed. Though I knew my husband would want me to be happy again, it took me a full two years before I finally decided to venture out of my comfort zone and give dating a try. As I dressed for my first date, my Catholic upbringing made me feel the need to go to confession. "Bless me Father, for I am about to sin. It has been fifty-two years since my last date."

Telling my daughters that I was about to have my first date was quite a thrill, and I know they were also having their own flashbacks. I am sure their wild youth came rushing back. I could hear them think, *What will Mom do on a date? After all, she's our mother, grandmother to our children. She's not some teenager. Just how far will mom go?* What fun I had watching the wheels of life turn in a different direction.

As I stood in front of the mirror, ready to leave the house for my first senior date, I honestly admit that I felt young and alive for the first time in a long while. My body was in fairly good shape and my spirit was willing. It was time. I felt awkward, but I paused, took a deep breath, and knew I was taking the first step towards the rest of my life.

Prepare!

Remember that the first date with any man is a learning experience. Before you go on that date, it may help to make a list of things you would like to find out about him. This can really help, especially if you are nervous, hesitant, or have a naturally quiet nature.

Review the personality traits and topics that are important to you, review the interests he listed on his profile, and, above all, remember his name! (Have you ever called a man by the wrong name? I have!) Be extremely careful if you are seeing more than one man at a time. I once left a message on a man's answering machine when I returned his call, and I used the wrong name. I was so embarrassed when he called back and corrected me! I hoped he knew it was an innocent mistake.

Pick a meeting place where you can relax and talk. Theater and movies can be wonderful if your interests lie in that direction, but before you go, spend some time getting to know each other. Having dinner first is always a good idea. Ask him about hobbies and inquire about books he likes to read or the wine he prefers to drink.

Much more will come to the surface in person than from the computer or a telephone conversation. A hint is to have a carefully chosen ice-breaker—a subject you know will animate him. Of course, once you walk into the restaurant and see Mr. Wonderful, all those questions may vanish from your mind.

One bit of advice that may be surprising: *Always thank a man when he compliments you.* Too many of us ignore the compliment, or we have slid into the state of mind that tells us, "I don't deserve it." Yes, you do! And he wants to know you're listening.

Make notes when you get home about your conversation while his words and your impressions are fresh. Did he arrive on time? Note how he dressed—did you like his style?

I didn't follow these rules to the letter myself. Before I started dating, I worried about how I could end a date that was not going well. I plotted with my daughters to call my cell phone at an appointed hour. If I didn't care for my date, I would suddenly have a family emergency and politely excuse myself. I thought it was more believable than a fake migraine headache.

In hindsight, I was not only rude, I was too quick on the trigger and cut too many dates short. I didn't give some of these gentlemen a fighting chance to get to know me, or for me to really know them.

I was *so* busy disqualifying my dates! My laundry

list was a mile long. My dates were too short, too tall, wore the wrong shoes, had no belt and didn't tuck their shirts in, and my list went on and on. Hair was important to me; whether long or short, it had to be neat. Eyebrows made me crazy, and nose hairs were a definite turnoff.

I have had lunch or dinner with men who constantly accepted cell phone calls, business or otherwise. I feel it's discourteous and just wrong. Answering his calls tells me he is more interested in his callers than in me. The same goes for you—if it's not a true emergency, your caller can wait. Turn off your ringer, at least through your meal, and focus on learning about the person sitting across the table from you. Excuse yourself and go to the restroom if you *must* check your cell phone.

The date itself

When I first began dating, I had more dates than I could keep up with. My daughters began referring to me as the one-date-wonder.

Sometimes I had a date with one man for coffee in the morning, one for lunch, and a different man for dinner. I was busy having fun, and deep down I hoped one of them would be my new Mr. Right. Looking back, I realize there were many kind, generous, and caring men with wonderful character

> *I've been on so many blind dates, I should get a free dog.*
> **—Wendy Liebman**

traits and loving hearts who might have been perfect for me.

Something had to change and that something was me. I was impatient and judgmental.

I was also obsessed in finding Mr. Tall, Dark and Handsome. After all, that is what I had all my life, so he should be easy to find the second time around. Well, guess again. No one was as tall, as tanned or as handsome as the fine man I had been married to for over fifty years.

Some of my best dates *were* unexpected surprises; they didn't fit my perfect man or perfect body concept, but we still had fun. This wasn't the norm, though. I tried hard to like each new man, but few made it to that important third date.

Still, sometimes it truly *is* impossible to connect with a date. No matter how hard you try to like the man on that first date, you can't relate to him and wishful thinking won't make it so. You've done your best to draw him out, and the conversation is going nowhere. You realize that though the face across the table appeals to you, there is no common link and there never will be.

If you are convinced that giving him a second chance would never change your mind, politely say *thank you*, and move on to the next candidate. It's hard but important to send him a text or email; say with kindness, "Thank you for lunch, but unfortunately, we are not a match." Even better, if you are brave enough, pick up the phone and give him the courtesy of a call.

Don't put added stress on yourself about how much affection you should show on your first date; we'll discuss sex in more detail later in the book. You may struggle over what to wear or what to say, but affection will come naturally.

Even in today's modern world, there's nothing wrong with a nice handshake and *thank you* at the end of the date. Simon and Garfunkel did a great song back in the Sixties that has an appropriate line, "Slow down, you move too fast . . ."

A kiss is often a natural gesture. Many of us feel that a kiss can help solve the mystery of the person on the receiving and giving end of the kiss. Unfortunately, kissing seems to have become a lost art.

If you are serious about looking for a romantic partner, you may have to kiss a lot of frogs before you find a prince.

No doubt you will think about the first kiss with someone new. I know I did! I thought: *When do I return a kiss and how warmly? What do I touch* and what's not a good idea to touch? Do I keep my mouth open or closed? What happens if his tongue creeps into my side of the kiss? When it feels right, natural things just happen, and all your questions will be answered.

Take your time! Kiss slowly; close your eyes and remember the emotions of your youth. You will feel romantic before you know it. Short or tall, stout or slim, if he is your Prince Charming, the kiss will be good from the first touch of your lips. They call that *chemistry*.

If he is quite interested in you, a man may do his best to snap you up on the first date and take you off the market and out of the dating pool. If you come close to his ideal of a perfect woman, he won't waste time and let you get snatched away by someone else. The flowers may start to show up, along with a gift or two.

The atmosphere of your first date sets the tone for your evening, but it can also mask the real person. Listen to his words and pay attention to his actions. They speak louder than the venue of your date.

When he takes you onto his sailboat and spends the afternoon complaining about his multiple divorces and how he supports all his ex-wives, you are in trouble right from the start. When he invites you to an elegant restaurant to impress you, but hands you the check, I suggest you run for the hills.

You may find your lifestyles and interests are *not* compatible. You may become so excited by mutual interests when you're talking on the phone—*so* sure you found your Mr. Right—that you start dreaming about the future before you even meet him. I did, more than once.

Guess what! Your prospective heartthrob may not like you or your ideas when he meets you, and you may realize you don't like him, either.

Who pays?

Most seniors live on fixed incomes. I certainly do, and I'm aware that dating is an expensive proposition for whoever picks up the check. If he leaves the first date options up to you, ask if he has any preferences. In any case, I recommend you never pick one of the more expensive restaurants in town.

Though one very handsome, well dressed gentleman clearly wasn't in financial distress, he was downright cheap. While he suggested expensive restaurants, he always insisted on choosing what we ate and splitting the meal to keep the costs down. (He did allow me to order one glass of wine.) By the third date, this big spender was off my dating list.

Never Too Late to Internet Date

Many men who are watching their expenses will opt for meeting in a coffee shop; some prefer breakfast, and some prefer lunch, happy hour, or early dinner. Since I'm somewhat of a date snob, if the man suggests a coffee shop, I suggest Starbucks. Coffee is almost five dollars; if you add a pastry and he gives you a funny look, offer to pay for the pastry and see his response. If he accepts your offer, I suggest you finish your pastry and go directly home, open your computer, and search for another match.

As we seniors all know, happy hours are very popular with the over-sixty crowd; they're a bit more glamorous than early bird specials and still affordable. I have gone to many happy hours on a first date and had very enjoyable evenings. Be flexible and let him lead, at least in the beginning.

One highly educated man had a profile that truly impressed me, and I looked forward to our date. We met for the first time at a happy hour, had two soft drinks (no cocktails) and shared an appetizer. When we were ready to leave, he said, "Dating sites are encouraging couples to split the check these days, and I agree. Your half of the bill including tip is $7."

I sure hadn't read *that* news on any site *I'd* investigated.

Modern Dating Do's and Don'ts

If we had gone to a very elegant restaurant, I would have offered to pay my share of the check, but I didn't see that happening with a fourteen-dollar happy hour bill. I looked him squarely in the eyes, said sweetly and firmly, "I don't split checks," and left the table. He didn't follow me.

Don't waste time worrying if you should pay for the date! That may sound insensitive, but if a man can't afford to spend less than $20 on a date, he shouldn't invite someone to join him for a meal. I feel that a woman should *absolutely* be treated on the first date.

Though I may be a bit more old-fashioned than some of you readers, I really do believe that the man should pay on all dates he instigates. In my view, going Dutch is for friends and business associates, not for dates. You are his guest. If he does ask you to pay, move on.

You can also pay in other ways. The most popular is to cook for him. Single men love a home-cooked meal. If he is the one who'll do the cooking, offer to do the grocery shopping. Be aware, though, if he asks you to dine at his home, he may be implying he expects sex, even on the first date. If you like him and the situation suits you, go for it.

You can also treat him to a movie. Order the tickets online, buy the big bag of popcorn, and surprise him with a bag of chocolate-covered raisins once you get settled in the theater. It gets them every time. Have you tried the new theaters with the lounge seating? If you haven't, it's an experience you'll both love! Usually the arms between the seats can be pushed up so you can hold hands.

If there is a special event you would like to attend, invite him to accompany you and offer to buy the tickets.

You can arrange and pay for outdoor adventures, dinners, and all types of events. The key difference is that he is *your* guest.

If you travel together, often expenses are shared. It's important to discuss expectations and budgets in advance. You can share the fun and not break the bank.

Caveats and expectations

Be aware: When a man mentions in his profile that he wants an organized woman, you had best be a clean and tidy person. If your house is a disaster, think twice before you invite him home (and think hard before you go out with him at all).

Popular first-date advice is to drive your own car to meet your date because you may need to make a sudden exit. Another way to keep your independence on a first date is to arrive via Uber

Modern Dating Do's and Don'ts

or another ride-share app. You can always choose to let him drive you home if you feel comfortable at the end of your date.

For dinner, *I* prefer a later seating because it's usually quieter. In today's world of noisy, trendy restaurants, it's hard to find a place you can really talk and hear the other person across the table.

There's a well-known dance bar in my town that everyone refers to as the desert's happening place, and it's known for its "party time." My youngest daughter took me there one evening to show me the sights, and I was thrilled to see men and women of all ages dancing and having a wonderful time. At a relaxed place like this, a man will ask to buy you a drink and invite you to dance. It's a great way to make new connections and a fun way to get back into the swing of dancing and socializing. You can approach a man, flirt, hold eye contact, talk if you can hear each other, and suddenly two strangers are dancing. You can become friends in a matter of minutes.

On weekends, the place is packed, with a line outside the door. My glamorous forty-something daughter and I were ushered right in. "Mom, find a bar stool and look interesting," she told me. *How does one look interesting*, I wondered, *especially at my age*! But I did as I was told, sat down, and sure enough, a nice gentleman asked me to dance. Guess I looked interesting.

In a place like this, sometimes men stand along the side, a bit afraid to approach you. Their body language says they would like to dance, but they hesitate. If you are brave, *you* do the asking. I danced several times while my daughter was offered multiple exciting proposals by men of all ages.

Find somewhere to go in your town and you might just be asked to dance by Mr. Wonderful. Women can now do the asking. After all, this *is* 2018. So why sit home?

Carry business cards with your name, phone number, and email address when you go out; leave off your address for safety issues. A card makes a good impression and shows an air of sophistication when you are browsing through the candy store of men. It never hurts to have one handy for the man who asks you for that second or third dance. You can print them at any office supply store and they are very affordable.

The more I dated, the more I became accustomed to meeting men. Each time, it became easier to get in my car, start the engine and drive to meet someone new. As my confidence grew, my ability to sort the men from the boys improved, and I trusted my instincts more. As a woman who is no raving beauty yet gets asked out on a regular basis, I feel it's because I've learned how to make a man feel comfortable and good about himself.

My dating adventures introduced me to wonderful and intriguing men. I have been offered trips to Europe, vacations in Hawaii, and many weekend get-a-ways. I never accepted any of the offers; I guess that I still felt bound by some of the more conservative rules of my youth.

That also may very well be why I am still unattached! I refused offers that down deep I would have loved to accept. Pressure from family and friends most certainly influenced my decisions. A dear friend's husband called my decisions "ladylike and honorable." I told him, "Thanks," and I did feel honorable, but was that what I *really* wanted when I crawled into bed alone night after night? I knew I wanted more, I just didn't know how to ask.

I look back now and wish I had done some of the fun things that were offered to me while I was a few years younger. I wish I could have been braver and accepted the many opportunities I was offered. Some I passed up because I wasn't sure the man was the right man for me. I should have tried harder to like each one. I am sure, looking back, that I could have reached out more often.

I learned that we also need to project confidence

to the person sitting across the table. When he smiles at you and his face lights up, it is because you are making him happy. Men, just like women, are looking for all the happiness they can find. Now they are suddenly finding that happiness on the internet.

Please don't give up on your internet dating site because of one bad date. I have friends who pay their money, take a look, try one date, and never give it another chance. Regretfully, there are also some who never get up enough courage to respond to a single man who contacts them. This is a pity, because someone wonderful may be right around the corner. If a date doesn't make a good fit, move on and hope the next person will be "the one."

We need the closeness of others, *especially* as we get older. Companionship has been scientifically proven to keep us younger, happier, and better functioning. Children and grandchildren most certainly have a place in our lives, but it is wonderful to have a hand to hold as you watch your evening television show or walk along the beach.

Be prepared to tell your date what you are looking for in a relationship. Some men will ask on the first date (or even during your first communications) what you expect to find—a friend, a good time, a companion, love, or a life partner? I like to know

Modern Dating Do's and Don'ts

a man before I'm willing to share my expectations, because they may vary depending on the man. Many women do have unyielding expectations; if you're one, it's probably fair to share them in your profile, right up front.

It can be difficult to come up with the words to describe your true desires to someone on the other side of a computer screen. Don't be shocked if a man comes right out and asks if you, as a senior woman, are still interested in sexual relations.

Though I'm no longer shocked, I am still surprised whenever a man asks about my sex drive on the first date. Recently, a man earnestly told me about his penile implant and great sex drive, though he was eighty. Did I really need to know this on our first date, between my wedge salad and grilled salmon entrée?

It's true that men put women in two categories. The first category is for women they play with, as in first-date sex or a friends-with-benefits situation, and the second category is for the woman he considers potential relationship material. He may figure he doesn't have enough time left to find out your interests through more subtle methods.

You are probably doing the same categorizing, though perhaps less blatantly. The person across the table may become better looking the more you get to know him. His laughter, bald spot, and love handles may start to become endearing and even sexy. Sometimes you just need to give him a chance.

And, sometimes, *you don't*!

A very charming doctor gave me a two-hour monologue about his career highlights and his famous professional children, and he never asked about *my* interests or *my* children. Lawyers, I have found, tend to do the same thing.

Talk to each other, don't preach. We all need to come down from our former professional pedestals, women and men alike, and begin communicating about what we do now. Our past lives are just that, our past.

Sometimes, our well-meaning children do some preaching of their own. They can make or break the best of relationships, and many times they intervene on behalf of their parent. I have more than one friend whose children had to stop them from lavishing gifts of cars and computers and big screen televisions on unscrupulous men who were taking advantage.

On the other hand, our children can be too protective and even break up a potential relationship if they feel threatened.

6

Getting Ready for the Bedroom

*In my sex fantasy,
nobody ever loves me for my mind.*
—**Nora Ephron**

If you were faithful to one man all your married life, and the only man who has seen you naked lately is your OB/GYN, the thought of sex with someone new can be intimidating. Still, most of us do miss the sexual companionship and energy of a man, and we seek the comfort of a warm body in an otherwise empty bed.

Healthy women and men can enjoy fulfilling sex well into their seventies and eighties. When older women say they have stopped wanting sex, even though it had been an important part of their married life, I always ask, "*Why*?"

Why *is* this? Most women blame pain, discomfort, and menopause. If you say you lost your sexual appetite due to what we refer to as the change of life, you didn't need to. You *let* it change your life. Hormone replacement therapy is available in tablets and creams, and there are many different types of suitable lubricants available at your local drug store.

Our biggest erogenous zone—our minds!—is between our ears. A doctor will tell you that no one gives anyone else an orgasm. An orgasm happens when conditions are right. You can wake up every day, happy, fulfilled, and unashamed that you've had as many orgasms as you desire with the help of your partner, a vibrator, or a fantasy. I've read that doctors recommend at least one orgasm per week and preferably three.

Are you surprised? You shouldn't be. Orgasms are good for us, psychologically and physically, no matter how we get them.

If you're thinking about re-entering the world of active sexual relations, it will help if you make sure your body is sexually awakened and responsive. Don't ask Mr. Right to find your switches all by himself in the dark when that special night finally arrives. You'll both have a much better experience

Getting Ready for the Bedroom

if you make sure your switches are already turned on.

By your third date, most people will know whether the bedroom is an option. When the moment of decision finally comes, it's natural for you to do a bit of soul-searching, but if the relationship feels good, *relax*. Give sex a chance. Always be honest, though. Don't fake anything, especially an orgasm.

Though erotica and sex toys weren't part of everyday conversation when we were brought up, things have changed. Most adults who are sexually active have no hesitation in getting a little help when they want to recharge their sex lives.

There are some amazing sex aids today for men and women, to use alone or together. The sheer variety available will put a smile on your face and make you more curious than you might expect.

When you get up your courage to make your first trip to the neighborhood adult toy shop, you might pray that you don't see anyone you know inside, especially your next-door neighbor. Instead, don't be ashamed! Take a couple of good friends with you, because it can be a wild and fun experience if you have never shopped in an adult/erotica store. The clerks, most of them women, will make you feel comfortable and help with great recommendations.

For my first trip, I went with two longtime friends after we had lunch with a second glass of wine for liquid courage. Those two glasses loosened us up all right, enough so we giggled our way through the store. We had great fun that afternoon and laughed all the way home.

If you prefer to do your toy shopping in private, there are a myriad of sites available, even Amazon.com. If you have an Amazon Prime account, expect free delivery, maybe even the next day. The order comes right to your door in a discreet, unmarked package.

Many of us were taught to ignore our vaginas, and we aren't informed about ways to keep this vital part of our body maintained, other than the usual hygiene routine. We moisturize our skin, but we ignore the part of our bodies that can really put a smile on our faces. You can avoid sexual discomfort and even pain if you consider vaginal moisturizers and lubricants; discuss them with your doctor. Some are prescription, and some of those include hormones. Even over-the-counter lubricants can make intercourse much easier and more enjoyable for both parties.

Men say that we women should tell them what we want in the bedroom, yet many of us don't have a clue how to start this conversation. It doesn't

Getting Ready for the Bedroom

need to be awkward, and it can be *very* rewarding to talk about the ways you desire intimacy with someone new. The discovery process becomes an important part of foreplay with a new partner. Talking about sex and what you like can be a great turn-on by itself.

Don't be afraid to share what you have learned about your body and your needs with your partner. Most men are exceptionally accommodating and want to make you completely happy.

Many men also need more help than you remember from the last time you had sex with someone new. You will need more patience and understanding than you did when you and your date were both in your twenties. Most men will show up prepared for sex, with a trusty condom in their pocket, and they now also pack little blue or yellow pills, perhaps even a shot or a pump. Senior men still have the same sexual equipment they did when they were young, but often things don't work as well as they'd like.

Spontaneity is no longer a part of the sexual act for most aging men. Men by the millions find themselves soft where they would prefer to be hard. You should be proud of a man who knows his body and is willing to use assistance to satisfy you and himself. Adapt the Boy Scout motto: *Be prepared.*

Since many men can't sustain an erection for a long period of time, also be prepared to seize the opportunity when it arises.

Remember that there are two things most senior men can't bear losing: their erection and their driver's license.

Sometimes you might need to set the stage to help the situation along. Put out candles, prepare dinner at home, and pray that when he sees the ambiance, he will want to skip dinner and head straight to dessert—you! Snuggling on the couch, relaxing outside on the patio, or holding hands while taking a walk can all lead to a romantic moment. Dancing and touching your partner can bring back feelings that stir the heart and get your libidos in high gear. Be creative; this is the time for you to shine.

> *The age of a woman doesn't mean a thing. The best tunes are played on the oldest fiddles.*
> **—Ralph Waldo Emerson**

Protection

I think every woman has fantasized about an incredible night of amazing sex with a new partner or lover, but buyer beware! You may get more than you bargained for. No matter how sexy the man,

Getting Ready for the Bedroom

you need to take precautions. Though he may show you the best orgasms of your life, you do not want to wake up in the arms of Mr. STD (STD=sexually transmitted disease).

The same is true for a man. Let's say he meets a woman, and she's so exciting he can't wait to take her to bed. If she is that willing, do you honestly think she has been a virgin all her life? If your date has unprotected sex with her, he may bring you souvenirs from that passionate encounter, plus some from all his and her previous partners.

Anyone can have a sexually transmitted disease, male or female, and it's not just transmitted by one-night-stands. They're *not* passed on by toilet seats as some people fear, and (almost never) by deep kissing, but almost always by sexual relations, which can mean oral sex or anal sex as well as vaginal intercourse.

Sexually transmitted diseases and infections (STDs and STIs) are on the rise among seniors. Many apparently believe "protection" refers to protection from pregnancy, and once they're past child-bearing years, they no longer need to worry. Unfortunately, they still do need to take precautions.

Sexually active adults can no longer plead ignorance, or admit to a dislike of "rubbers," or say protection isn't necessary because they can't get pregnant. We may have been lucky when we were young, and there weren't quite as many varieties of STDs then. HIV didn't come along until the 1980s.

Only one in six sexually active single adults over fifty reports using a condom on a regular basis, according to the CDC, the Center for Disease Control.

Every man has an opinion on condoms. Some men will refuse to use a condom; they say they don't have any feeling if they put one on. Perhaps they're talking about GI-issue condoms from their days in the service; these days excellent varieties of condoms allow for full sensation. Have they tried them?

A man once confided to me he couldn't get hard enough to put on a condom. What did he do? He had unprotected sex in a Las Vegas hotel room with a stranger, indulging in a very dangerous night. Fearing the worst, he went to the doctor and was tested. He was lucky that time and came away unscathed, but the result could have been disastrous. There are many men who've done something that stupid, and they may be on your dating site.

We all want to have a healthy sex life, so how do we gracefully and safely handle the most serious issue to come down the pike for sexually active seniors? If you can't comfortably talk about safe sex with your potential partner, how can you possibly trust them inside your body? It's your call on this issue, but please don't shy away from the subject.

I guess this means, ladies, that we better go out and buy some condoms. Better yet, take your fellow to a sex shop and shop for condoms together; you will be amazed at the different flavors and textures they offer. You might even find a new toy before you exit the shop.

Ladies, don't *ever* feel too embarrassed to carry your own condoms in your purse.

I did quite a bit of research on STDs and STIs, and I found some eye-opening information. I don't want to distract you right now, but please take the time to read the appendix at the back of the book **before** you begin a sexual relationship with someone new.

Senior sex 101

Affection and sex are different with every man and woman, often ending up in ways that you would not have expected. We all know there are many methods of satisfying each other, and the size and firmness of a man's penis doesn't have to dictate the quality of his lovemaking skills. You will need to find your comfort level under the sheets, and it will be an adjustment for both of you.

A worthwhile one, though!

Get into bed, take a deep breath, keep an open mind, and enjoy yourself. Sex will become less stressful if you can accept your body as it is now, and accept the unfamiliar feel of a taller, shorter, bonier, or perhaps rounder body next to you. A caring, sexual man will enjoy the moment, put you at ease, and do his best to make you very happy.

You may need to change your preferred sexual positions due to his or your physical limitations. Yes, you can adjust and find brand-new ways to pleasure one another. Keep plenty of extra pillows on hand for all those sore joints you've both accumulated over the years.

Sex in the afternoon when you are both rested can be a wonderful, spontaneous event. Think of all the times when you were a young parent and the children knocked on the bedroom door. Those worries are over, and we are now lucky senior citizens. Take the phone off the hook and enjoy your new sexual freedom.

Be careful if you plan to be creative in the shower, and make sure there's a well-anchored grab bar. Before you get into a bathtub to take a very romantic bubble bath together, be confident you can actually climb out of the tub.

Getting Ready for the Bedroom

I know you are laughing by now, and that's good, because it means you've experienced and survived awkward situations in the past. If we can't laugh at ourselves, how we can finally be free of all the hang-ups we have collected over the years?

We all go through the same issues as we age. It's just uncomfortable to discuss them, especially with a new friend of the opposite sex. How many senior issues do you bring to the bedroom?

Snoring may come into play on both sides of the mattress. Sleep apnea at any age can become a bothersome issue. One of you may need a CPAP machine that runs all night, but that's better than snoring.

How about an oxygen tank that goes off and on a hundred times throughout the night? Or do you think you'll lie awake trying to remember if you took your bedtime pills, but don't want to get out of bed and disturb the man lying next to you?

Topics like bladder control can be awkward to deal with at first, as well, but they shouldn't. Be reassured that urgency, frequency, and occasional leaks affect both men and women after a certain age. Most men over 65 have at least some prostate issues, and childbirth and gravity have had their way with most women.

Do you worry about what happens if his

equipment doesn't work? Relax, and help him relax. It may be nerves and performance anxiety, and it may be something more permanent. He may need some help, and usually the first step is trying Viagra or a similar drug. Viagra has been around since 1998 and has helped men of all ages. The little blue pill has made "erectile dysfunction" a part of everyday conversation, and more than twelve million prescriptions were written last year alone. Soon, the pills will become generic and very affordable, possibly even sold over the counter.

Sometimes, unfortunately, even the little blue pills don't always work.

It is just as hard for a man to accept his aging body as it is for a woman. Many men have gone through prostate issues and have seen their testosterone level decline, which directly affects their sexual ability.

One of the new and innovative treatments is called Low T Therapy—testosterone that might be injected, implanted, or absorbed through a patch. It's not a silver bullet, but it can help many men.

A recent University of Chicago study found that one third of men aged 50 to 64 suffer from erectile dysfunction, and it rises to approximately 44 percent for the 65-to-85 age group. The statistics also say only half of those men will ever seek treatment. It's the natural process of aging, but many men are too proud to admit they even have an issue.

Erectile dysfunction is more than just the quality of an erection; it can involve arousal, length of time required to become erect, and recovery times.

Men at age fifty can get an erection in zero to five minutes, but by age sixty-five, it may take twenty to thirty minutes to become erect (and even then it might not be what they hope for). As they grow older, most men need more stimulation to become aroused. Still, pleasure belongs to anyone who is willing to create it. There are many options, and no one should have to live without an orgasm. A man doesn't need an erection to have an orgasm, and he doesn't need an erection to give the woman an orgasm, either.

Men hung up on their virile pasts should instead decide it's time to make creative love, rather than have "vanilla" sex. Senior sex should not be centered solely on vaginal intercourse; there are many fulfilling alternatives, and many ways to find pleasure.

Most women need and desire to be stimulated by a hand or mouth, whether the man has an erection or not. Quite a few senior women don't miss the penis at all, and they quickly learn to prefer the alternatives. A man can do wonderful things with the rest of his body, and the chances are he will know just what to do. Enjoy him the way he is and don't expect him to be a young stud. The time for young sex is over.

There are ways to set the stage hours before you have sex, actions you can take that will pique your partner's imagination and allow him to start the arousal process in advance. Call him the day of your date; give him the sexy details of what you want to do that evening. Arrange for a couple's massage that afternoon. Plan for an evening of kissing and cuddling in front of the fireplace. Get a sexy movie on Netflix. Let your imagination go wild.

You wouldn't need to help his libido if he was twenty, but it can make a difference now.

What we seniors worry about as we begin dating again! True, most of the things that make us nervous now are the same things that worried us when we were young. Still, whoever says *"age is just a number"* never had an internet date.

7

SEX AND SLEEPOVERS

If you obey all the rules, you miss all the fun.
—**Audrey Hepburn**

$\mathcal{W}$e know intimacy plays a large role in any relationship, but how do we choose our first romantic experience with someone other than our husband or life partner? Ideally, you make the choice gradually, as you get to know the person. From the first email to the time you take off your clothes, you will be peeling away layers of intimacy and learning to trust him.

Don't rush it. The decision is up to you. No matter how you face intimacy the first time with a new partner, it should be when *you* are ready. If you think you will regret it, do as Nancy Reagan would: *Just say no.* You should have sex when *you* feel connected, and your partner makes you feel wanted and desired.

When I first started to date, I questioned my judgment: *When is the right time? How will I know he's the right man? Should we know each other better or longer? What will the neighbors think of a strange car in my driveway all night?* Silly thoughts, perhaps, but serious to me and many others.

> *Make love when you can.*
> *It's good for you.*
> —**Kurt Vonnegut**

I have always taken control of my life, and I would *never* have sex with someone just because he asked. I know that when some men want to get close to you, sex is the only way they know how.

Throughout all my dating experiences, I've never climbed into any bed I didn't want to, and I've never been talked into sex against my better judgment. I'd been close many times, but I stood my ground. Sex on first dates is not an option for me, either, because I've always needed more connection than a first date usually allows.

If *you're* ready for a sexual experience on the first date, go for it.

Sex is for two, and thoughtful men feel the responsibility to satisfy both themselves and you. Most men are aware of your needs and pleasures,

Sex and Sleepovers

and they want you to enjoy sex as much as they do, if not more.

Yet, some men *are* very selfish, and it applies to their sex lives, too. They'll take just what they want, and they'll put the responsibility of both their performance and yours onto *your* shoulders. Some men will have their orgasm, roll over and go to sleep, leaving the woman not completely satisfied and wanting more.

Let's talk about sexual desire. *Merriam-Webster* defines *lust* as pleasure, craving, and intense desire. Once you are headed to the bedroom, you have crossed the line to the sheets, so prepare yourself.

Here's the bottom line about sex: *Just do it!* With practice, you will become more relaxed and comfortable. You may wonder about who does what to whom, and the feel, smell, and taste of their body may be different, but sex is like riding a bicycle. Climb on, and I can almost guarantee you'll get where you were headed.

It may seem strange to look over and see a new man's head on the pillow next to you, but it is easier than you think.

Should you be "easy," as men used to say?

Many men believe that adult dating *always* means sleeping together, especially after a few dates. These men think if they're sexually attracted to you, sex is the natural outcome. Some described it as an itch that you just need to scratch. In the game of love, it is easy to capture his penis; it's just hanging around waiting for an invitation. But capturing his *heart* . . . that's the challenge.

My friend Jan calls sex "emotional glue," but the simple truth is sometimes the glue doesn't stick. You must realize, just because you have sex with someone, it doesn't mean you are in a serious relationship.

My longtime friend Kat admitted that she invited her date back to her home on a first date. Within 30 minutes of finishing their first meal together, they were both naked in bed. Sadly, Kat never heard from him again. He got what he wanted and moved on. I was surprised by her candor, but I shouldn't have been. Many lonely women want the closeness of a man as soon as they can get one in their sights.

My college roommate, Phyllis, confided to me that though she wasn't looking for romance, she had been determined to have sex again before she died. She started her hunt on an internet dating site a few years earlier and liked it *so* much and was *so* successful that she decided playing the field was a better choice than entering a committed relationship. To this day, she hasn't settled down with one man. Great sex starts with an honest attitude, and Phyllis most definitely had one.

There are many chances to meet the right person online, and when he appears, don't hesitate too long. When the wrong one shows up, you'll know that, too. Trust your instincts.

Sleepovers

To stay or not stay overnight? That's the $64,000 question: When is the right time?

Once you've had sex with a man and are ready for more intimacy, a sleepover is the next step in your relationship. Inviting someone for a sleepover is a sign of trust. A sleepover gives you a great deal of private time to know the person on the other side of the pillow. An invitation to stay over says you're interested in going a little deeper than a brief sexual encounter allows.

Many women don't have a problem with sleepovers, but when I first began dating, I couldn't imagine asking a man to spend the night. Then I met a special man whom I will call Steve.

He was a delightful, sexy gentleman, twice married and a dating pro, He took my hand and gently guided me back to feeling things I thought I'd never experience again. At the end of a very romantic evening, I didn't know enough to ask him to stay the night. The "car in the driveway" phobia was running through my head.

I didn't understand the importance of a sleepover.

When I finally found the courage a few weeks later and invited Steve to spend the night, he declined and said he was busy. I soon learned he was busy spending the night with another woman, one who was a little *easier*.

A sleepover doesn't always have to involve sex, but it still implies a certain level of confidence in your relationship. While I was visiting friends in Orange County, I met Paul, a very charming man, and we had dinner. At the end of our date I had some doubts about his intentions as he pressed me against his chest, kissed me good night, and asked if my breasts were real. I laughed and responded, "I didn't have to buy them."

When Paul asked me to his beach front home the next day, I thought about his good night kiss, but decided to give him the benefit of the doubt. We sat on the sand, talking about our past work lives and our families. We had a great time and had a tremendous amount in common. The day flew by, and I felt we had really connected.

As the evening grew late, Paul casually asked me to spend the night. He said his intentions were honorable, and they very well may have been, but the guest room was right next to the master bedroom. I felt awkward because I had met him only the day before, and it seemed too soon. I weighed my feelings of trust against the strong liking I felt for him, and propriety won out—I politely declined.

I never heard from Paul again.

Many women would have jumped at his offer. A beautiful home, a polite, handsome man. Was I wrong? Paul had all the bells and whistles a woman would want, but I held back. I look back now and question myself. What would *you* do in this situation? Would I act differently today? Maybe.

8

An Affair (Not) to Remember

*Never regret. If it's good, it's experience.
If it's bad, it's an experience.*
—**Victoria Holt**

*W*hy can't we forget our first passionate, grown-up affair? Whether you are seventeen or seventy, I think the first time your heart flip-flops is one of the most exciting memories of our lives. We all long for that perfect "affair to remember."

Some people say you can only have an affair if you're married, but I disagree. Deborah Kerr and Cary Grant were both single in the movie *An Affair to Remember,* and the sparks were most certainly flying.

Maybe those chance romantic meetings and exciting love affairs only happen in the movies; I hope not. I want a romance just like that, and I am sure you do, too. The meeting of two individuals attuned to each other can be magical. I refer to them as *affairs*, and as special as they are, we can't forget them, even when we should.

When I think of *An Affair to Remember*, I think of a very nice widower I met on a cruise a few years ago. Michael and I enjoyed each other's company for the entire twelve days we spent on the ship. We were both a bit lonely, and we were so lucky to meet the first night at sea when we were assigned to the same dinner seating. We drank champagne, took long walks and gazed at the stars. San Francisco in the moonlight is a magical experience, especially when viewed from the ship's highest deck. We enjoyed each other's company, and both Michael and I felt we were protected, living in a bubble, a step away from real life.

Though I was filled with the romance of our cruise, I made the decision not to venture into a sexual affair. He was an east coast man, I was a California girl, and both of us were unsure how a long-distance affair would work out. We each wanted a long-term relationship, and a few nights in bed might have been fun, but it would have been a false promise.

An Affair (Not) to Remember

We said our good-byes dockside with one last hug and kiss. We never met again as we had fantasized on the ship; back in the real world, I had no regrets. It was an affair we both wanted to have, but we didn't take that next step.

A few months later, I met a truly wonderful man, a man I knew could become my Mr. Wonderful. I had been dating for two years, and at our first meeting, I knew Chuck was "the one."

He was a retired business man and widower who'd had a long marriage. We had so much in common and we were a great match—he even liked to dance in the kitchen! My attraction to Chuck was immediate. We took a brief trip together; I stayed with a friend and he stayed in a hotel. We had a wonderful time, even making out in the carwash like teenagers.

Chuck was visiting from out of town and planned to winter in my area. When he went back home to sell one of his residences, we stayed in contact. A few weeks later I received a very polite call from Chuck; he said he'd met someone in his home town and wanted to see where their relationship would go. I didn't know how to respond. I wished him good luck. What else could I do? The truth be told, I was devastated. He was the finest man I had met in my time on the internet dating circuit. He could have been the next love of my life, but he never gave me a chance.

I thought Chuck and I were perfect for each other, yet nothing sexual happened. It probably should have.

Would that have changed our relationship?

We had enjoyed each other's company and it was truly "an affair (I wanted) to remember," even though it was just my fantasy.

When my friends asked if I had heard from Chuck, I was only too happy to say his name and pretend down deep things could be different. They weren't.

Ironically, his relationship with the new woman from his home town didn't work out, and he called me, asking to be friends. I yearned to be more than just his friend, and I wasn't about to play second fiddle after having been in the first chair all my life.

> *Men always want to be a woman's first love; women like to be a man's last romance.*
> —**Oscar Wilde**

Chuck returned to town months later, yes, I saw him again, a difficult but necessary step for me to take before I could move on. We again spent time together and yes, the spark was still there, and we both knew it. This time, I allowed the spark to flame, but the moment it did, I realized an affair with Chuck wasn't what I wanted at all. Trust and respect had collided in the bedroom. I needed the whole package, and it wasn't there anymore. I thought I had found my Mr. Right, but he turned out to be Mr. Wrong.

I blamed myself for not being able to hold on to Chuck the first time around. The second time, I put the blame squarely on him and convinced myself that *I* didn't fail, things just didn't work out. After a bit of soul searching, I realized it wasn't his job to make me happy. I had to reach for happiness on my own.

You can give your body to someone, but don't expect them to desire it forever. They may, if the stars align, timing is right, and luck is on your side. In our search for lasting love, we must be prepared for the consequences, perhaps even a few tears.

Still, I did enjoy our brief encounter, and I highly recommend you cherish your own special affairs. If they don't work out, pick yourself up, dust yourself off, and start all over again.

Mark these good times as treasured memories and move on, and that is what I did. It didn't happen in a day, but it happened. So where did I go next? Right back to the internet.

The "L" word

Secretly, I think we all want a torrid love affair, but romance still comes first for most of us. Some of us try to convince ourselves that we're in love. What we're feeling in the glow of a new relationship may be the beginnings of love. On the other hand, it may be lust, or perhaps it's just the happiness of being with someone who's delightful and who obviously likes us, too.

Most romantic men and women enjoy the fantasy of being in love, and for them the words come all too quickly. Also, it's all too easy to convince yourself that you're in love to justify having sex, especially if you've had few sexual partners or been celibate for years. This is a mistake with serious consequences.

It *is* all too easy to get swept away; we can easily say and do things we think twice about the next day. Saying *I love you* may seem natural, but most men and women say too much, too soon.

I love you has consequences, and usually they're not what's intended. Words can frighten you or your prospective suitor away. Once those three words are out of your mouth, you can't take them back.

An Affair (Not) to Remember

Louis, a wonderful man, said *I love you* to me on our third date, yet by that point he'd only kissed me on the cheek (he was one of the rare men who made it to the third date). I thought, "How can he be in love with me? He hardly knows me."

From that moment, our relationship was doomed. Though he may have truly meant the words, they were said far too early in our dating relationship. I liked him, but I didn't know if I eventually would get to the point of love. I felt that had we continued dating after his declaration, I was leading him on, because love wasn't reciprocal. I gently broke our connection to avoid hurting him more in the long run.

There are many reasons people are premature with declarations of love. Sometimes we try to convince ourselves we're in love to justify our actions. You may look at dating like a do-over, a romantic second chance to replace an unhappy, unfulfilling marriage. *Especially* if that's your situation, don't move too fast with *I love you*.

Men say there are different levels of love; sometimes it may be just "convenient" love, or it may be genuine love. Capturing a person's heart can be a challenging experience. Even if you go to bed with someone and share their body, it doesn't mean you will ever hear *I love you* murmured by your partner.

Happily, love can happen at any time in your life. When it finally does, those three little words are priceless.

Senior dating quirks

You can become a serial dater, moving from person to person. We're all-to-quick to eliminate our dates for a variety of reasons. One reason that *sounds* silly (but it's not!) is bad kissing. Many women agree that men need to go back to kissing school and learn to make out all over again. Think of the fraternity parties you used to attend, and how you happily made out for hours.

If someone you're dating seems surprisingly anxious to get involved, don't let this scare you away. Many seniors fear their dating years are limited, and they feel a need to hurry and get a commitment. Some men feel time is of the essence—and they don't want to waste a moment.

On the other hand, there are some valid reasons to be leery. Some men have a strong need to be in full control of the relationship, and they can be turned off by someone who is obviously interested in them. These men arrange their lives so that there is no comfortable place for the woman in the relationship. The man assumes a reserved wait-and-see attitude, a cool keep-in-touch approach. After a while, they drift back into their dating pool, fish around, and move on to a new face.

If a man says he wants to play the field? *Believe him*. You aren't going to change his mind. If a man says he wants to date a variety of women, he will, even if you're convinced you're the best thing that ever happened to him. If he introduces you as his *friend*, know that is all you will ever be. If he really cared for you he would refer to you as his *girlfriend*, or perhaps by an affectionate name, some name that proves he's glad to have you in his life.

What if it's not passion that's driving him? Some seniors don't want to be alone as they age, and they're sure they'll feel more secure with a partner by their side. You'll hear that someone is looking for a "nurse and a purse;" it's a crass way to describe what they want, yet many men and women are hoping to find just that type of companion.

Woman say many senior men are looking for a place to live and a possible replacement for his wife, and if he is a survivor of a long marriage, that's often the case. It also can be a smart financial decision for both parties. At our age, marriage doesn't have to play the key role in relationships.

I encourage couples to live together, if it works

in your situation. Enjoy the fact that you have found someone to be with, and don't worry about the neighbors. Your family and friends will accept your relationship; anyone who doesn't, doesn't truly care about your happiness. If you enjoy each other's company, share some hobbies, and can develop mutual friends, your relationship can bring you a great deal of happiness.

You'll hear many instances of couples who move in together to enhance their financial security. Yes, it's true, two can live cheaper than one. I have many friends who live together for a combination of companionship, travel, sex, and yes, money.

> *Go confidently in the direction of your dreams. Live the life you have imagined.*
> **—Henry Thoreau**

Prepare for possible resentment from family members—yours and his. Children can be extremely protective of their parents, and family issues can be destructive to a relationship. Children worry about our financial future (and theirs), the house, bank accounts, and cars. They want to make sure it all stays in your name only. Children can present a hundred reasons why two seniors should not live together, and they may never even consider the benefits.

An Affair (Not) to Remember

In the long run, love will prevail, and you will do the right thing.

Friends with blended families can not only enhance their lives but keep themselves so busy with events they forget they are seniors. One dear couple I know has nine children between them, and too many grandchildren to count. My husband and I met them on a cruise; after three days of dinners and bridge they admitted that at the ages of 80 and 82 they were "living in sin." They share holidays and a happy round of graduations, weddings, and birthday parties. Being together is easy and fulfilling when both of you are accepted as a couple.

A few months ago, I was invited to Lynn's eightieth birthday party, a dear friend who had been dating Mitchell, a charming 81-year-old, for more than two years. When we stood to toast Lynn's birthday, she surprised the entire audience with the announcement that she and Mitchell were about to be married. As we stood there, jaws ajar, a minister appeared and performed the wedding ceremony.

Happiness can come at any age, and this mother, grandmother and great-grandmother is a perfect example of a woman who recognized this and seized the moment.

What happens if you are in a relationship and

it crumbles for no reason you can see? Betsy, an out-of-town friend, told all her friends she'd met a man, and swore to all of us that he was the most handsome, wonderful man she had ever dated. She was sure that Jack was "the one," and knew they were a perfect pair.

One night, Jack drove to her home to spend the night, or so told her. When he arrived, he didn't even sit down. He stood in front of Betsy and announced that the love of his life had just called him eight hours before; she wanted him back and planned to marry him.

Stunned, Betsy asked, "Why didn't you just call me? Do you think you're softening the blow by telling me in person?" Jack left without answering.

One week later, the love of his life called off their wedding, and Betsy saw Mr. Perfect hop back onto the dating site within a week without missing a beat. She wondered if the story was just that, a story and a way to dump her. Some men just go from woman to woman, hoping to find their perfect mate.

I can personally vouch for having had a disappointing relationship. *The only man I truly wanted was the only one I couldn't have.*

There isn't much that can be done when one of you decides it's over, other than to end the relationship gracefully. Of course, we all know that marriage or living together is no guarantee that a relationship will last forever. You may not understand why the break happened, and it may take many tears and a long time to recover, but this too will pass.

This is a good place to share my dear friend Suzie's favorite quote:

"I'd rather look back at my life and say, 'I can't believe I did that, than to wish, I never had done it at all.'"

I heard a delightful true story in a class that I took recently. The teacher's mother, who lives in a retirement community, walked up to an older gentleman at the common mailboxes. She asked him, pointblank, "Are you lonely?"

He answered honestly, "Yes, I'm very lonely. Will you join me for dinner tonight?" Three weeks later, they moved in together; she is eighty-five and he is ninety. Guess you are never too old to find love and happiness, even at the mailbox.

9

THE COWBOY

Life would be empty without stories... I write so the world never runs out of stories to share.
—Tinka Taylor

I have an affair to share with you.

My Cowboy story began while I was in Seattle, Washington, attending my best friend's wedding; she was marrying her third husband. Late on her wedding night, I sat alone at her kitchen table, browsing my dating site. Suddenly a very handsome cowboy appeared, or, shall I say, *rode* onto my laptop.

I've been a lifelong John Wayne junkie, even attended a fund-raising event at his house in Newport Beach, California. I will never forget touching his hand-carved saddle in the family room. John Wayne's presence was everywhere.

During my long marriage, my six-foot four-inch, two-hundred-thirty-five-pound husband was often referred to as a modern-day John Wayne by others. He always seemed larger than life, not only to his family but to his business associates and friends.

As I stared at the man who sat comfortably astride his horse, looking back at me from my computer screen, I felt instant attraction. Could he be my new John Wayne? I wrote to him and he answered right away, saying though he wasn't John Wayne, he sure wished he could be if that would attract me. Smooth.

The Cowboy's profile included my city, which was the reason he popped up on my site. Unfortunately, he was at his Nevada ranch, and here I was, Sleepless in Seattle. We were both traveling, miles from home, but searching our dating site to meet someone new. He planned to move to his winter residence in my town within a month and, amazingly enough, his ranch was within ten minutes of my home.

We talked on our cell phones non-stop the next few weeks while he roped cattle, tended his horses, and made his way to Southern California. He was charming, with an infectious laugh, part of his southern charm, and we became friends before we ever met. We talked for hours about our families, grandchildren, careers, marriages, and his multiple divorces.

We were worlds apart, and maybe that was the attraction for me. I had dated many men, but no one sparked my interest until the Cowboy. I was a widow with one long marriage, and he was a retired prosecutor with three ex-wives. Suddenly, I was playing the telephone waiting game, anxious for his call.

For our first date, he insisted on taking me out to dinner, anywhere I wanted to go. Dinner reservations were in place, and I was very excited to finally meet the man behind the voice.

At three o'clock that Friday afternoon, he was stuck in Los Angeles traffic, pulling his trusty horses over the California Ridge route, and I knew he couldn't possibly make the evening as planned. I suggested he come to my place for dinner instead.

My daughters thought I had lost my mind. I was inviting a stranger to my home for dinner for our first date, the biggest no-no of internet dating. I reassured them that at his age, which was the same as mine, and after an eight-hour trek towing his loyal steeds, I was certain he had to be harmless.

We settled on take-out pizza and salad from a local Italian restaurant, located halfway between both of our houses. I called in the order, and the Cowboy arrived, dinner in hand, some time later.

When I opened the door, I saw a handsome man, dressed more for a game of golf than a horseback ride, sporting a broad smile and carrying our take-out meal. He handed me a greeting card, a John Wayne card, with a cute hand-written message inside and had signed it, "The Duke." Oh, this man was good.

We talked like old friends who had not seen each other in a long while. I know we were both surprised by the immediate connection we felt.

I stared at him across the table and wondered, *Just who* is *this man*? His eyes were blue as a clear lake, his salt-and-pepper gray hair reached his collar and needed a trim. He looked like the perfect cowboy. By nine o'clock he was almost asleep at the table, and we called it a night. No kiss or hug, just a "Thank you, ma'am," and a hand shake at the door, just like John Wayne would do on a first date.

The next day, Cowboy called and asked me to a movie, a movie about lawyers, of course. We sat side by side like platonic buddies, and he never even reached for my hand. He was unshaven and looked like an unmade bed. I was losing interest fast, wondering if our numerous phone calls had been wasted time. I was disappointed in his

The Cowboy

appearance and decided I really didn't care if I saw him again.

Then the Cowboy asked me to go dancing. For the first time in a long while I had my arms around big, broad shoulders, and I liked it. I wasn't a very good dancer, but he was an excellent teacher. It was the beginning of my first dating romance.

I didn't quite fit in with the trendy ladies on the dance floor, so one of my daughters took me shopping to outfit me in more stylish clothes, down to the sequined silver shoes that matched the outfit. As we shopped together, I felt like a teenager and my confidence soared. Talk about role reversal! We left the store and my beautiful daughter turned to me, wrapped her arms around me, and whispered in my ear, "Mom, you really look hot." I really felt hot!

The next night, we had dinner at a local hotel, then danced under a large dimly lit tree in the moonlight outside the dining room. When we realized we had crashed someone's wedding reception, we blended into the crowd and kept dancing. What could be more romantic?

At a local dance club a few nights later, we were approached by a young woman who insisted we were the most adorable couple she had ever seen. *Still* when the night ended there was no goodnight kiss. The next night we shared a beer; I even sat at the bar, a first for me, and we danced and danced and danced.

As we sat on my patio a few nights later, listening to Rod Stewart sing the old standards and watching the sprinklers water the golf course, he reached for me, took me in his arms, and after two weeks and many dances, finally kissed me. When he did, I never wanted him to stop. He left very late that night.

My Cowboy spent every morning riding his horses and practicing his roping; he loved playing cowboy. Later, we would spend hours talking, reinventing the world, musing about someday writing a book to help seniors get over their hang ups and put them at ease with dating and relationships. When I look back, I think perhaps he was referring to me and my inexperience at dating.

If opposites really do attract, we were a prime example.

My two daughters met him, and they weren't pleased their mother was attracted to a wandering cowboy, even a retired, respectable one. When he asked me to take a trip to the east coast for a week to visit a family friend, my daughters were adamant that I "just say no." He was so different from the remarkable and dependable father who had raised them, and they were protective of their mother, naturally so, given the circumstances.

"Mother, you can't spend a week with a man you barely know!" They had many reasons why I shouldn't travel with him, so I listened to them and declined his invitation; after all, it was hard to defend his rambling lifestyle.

Those instances when I did try to incorporate him into my world, he was unavailable. I understood. He'd had a successful, extremely demanding law career, and all he wanted to do in retirement was to ride his horses. I felt he had earned that right.

When he returned from his travels, our fun continued. A couple of weeks later he again asked me to go away with him, this time to meet some of his horse friends in his LA riding club, just a weekend getaway. He even offered me a separate hotel room, just like I would expect John Wayne to do. Afraid to venture out of my comfort zone, I declined again. I had never been on a horse; knowing he would be surrounded by his friends made me more insecure about my own feelings. He, of course, went without me.

I was upset at myself for not accepting his invitations. I cared for him and kept telling myself all I wanted was fun, but what did I really want? Looking back now, I know I wanted fun on *my* terms.

Within a few weeks, we went from the dance floor, to the patio, to the couch, and then to the bedroom. We were two single adults, *so* different, who didn't fit together anywhere except in each other's arms. I didn't realize how much I'd missed passion.

He helped me reenter the world of intimacy; he knew all the tricks and just what buttons to push. I think he must have learned how to seduce a lady from all the old John Wayne movies he watched; after all, the Duke always won the girl.

He made me feel more confident, and better about myself. He gave me the gift of himself, and he didn't ask for anything in return except my satisfaction. He always focused on showing me the pleasure and joy of the moment. It was obvious he liked women, enjoyed sex and was happy to accommodate. The man never gave up.

Though I'd built a wonderful life with my husband, the Cowboy, all these many years later, was exciting and *"all* for me." Still, I was forced to admit his actual performance was limited. I tried to reassure him how very romantic he was, but he was one macho cowboy. He was beginning to face the realization that things didn't work as they had all his life. I asked him, "Is it me?" Of course, he told me I was wonderful, and just between us, I knew I was. I encouraged him to try the famous

The Cowboy

little blue pill, and I still smile when I remember him walking into the house shaking a bottle of blue pills.

A few weeks went by filled with movies, dinners, and lots of time spent in the bedroom, and then he announced he would be traveling to Las Vegas to attend the National Rodeo. This time, he didn't ask me to go along.

When he returned, I sensed things had changed. I could feel him slipping away, and I knew he must have found a new cowgirl somewhere along the trail. I had said *"No"* to his life style, and I still had much to learn about dating, relationships and single, sexy men (yes, he was one sexy man). Women usually bond with a man after sex, but a man's heart does not need to be connected to his penis when he is in a physical relationship. That's how they can walk away so easily.

We had been driving down a two-way street, and suddenly I was driving one way, alone. I finally realized that men make love to you one day, make no commitment, and can leave you the next. They are often handsome, extremely masculine, very self-indulgent and great fun, which described the Cowboy to a tee.

A week or two later he came over to help me decorate my Christmas tree. I watched as he placed my ornaments on the tree and could sense how uncomfortable he was. He politely asked where they came from, interested yet distant, and he didn't share stories of his own family's Christmas. My tree was adorned with wonderful family heirlooms. I sensed he didn't have special holiday memories of his own and didn't want to talk about his past.

Later that evening, after a romantic candlelit dinner, I asked him to spend the night and he declined. I knew our romantic interlude was finally over.

He called less and less. I am sure he sensed how hard it was for me to let go, and being the sensitive man I knew he was, he tried to let me down easy. He knew I didn't give myself lightly, but we just didn't fit. I wanted him to be someone he wasn't capable of being. He wanted to keep his roving life style; to this day, I'm not sure what I wanted from him.

I knew it wasn't to be forever, but I wasn't ready for it to end yet. Then one day he just stopped calling. He didn't break my heart, but it was bruised for a long time.

He is still riding his horses, I am still looking for Mr. Right, and we have friendly conversations and laugh every now and then. We're two stubborn Taurus individuals, yet whatever drove us apart has

The Cowboy

made us friends. We now consider our relationship as "friends with benefits." When we get together, we laugh at the fun times we shared, and yes, we laugh in bed. I can't seem to put him out of my mind, and to this day I can't explain why he stays. He still lives rent-free in my head.

Don't cry because it's over, smile because it happened.
—**Dr. Seuss**

Dating the Cowboy was not in vain. Though he wasn't my Prince Charming and he may never have been my Mr. Right, there will always be a special place in my heart for the Cowboy, *my* Cowboy. We shared a wonderful "Affair To Remember."

10

BOYS AND THEIR TOYS, AND THE GAMES THEY PLAY

A man's gotta do what a man's gotta do.
—**John Wayne**

Men who focus on impressing the women they want to date tend to dangle their toys in obvious ways. They may have two houses, a motor home, a boat, or very fancy cars, and they make sure you know about every shiny acquisition.

He who dies with the most toys wins seems to be their motto.

I have met more than a few men competing for top dog in those categories. They love to talk about all their stuff, but remember, it is just *stuff*.

You can identify them easily. They stand

proudly beside their favorite form of identity, usually their automobile or their golf cart. Their posts say they want a sweet woman, years younger than they are, interested in great sex, dive bars, and foreplay.

Fortunately, most men list more reasonable hobbies: going to movies and museums, attending the theater, playing cards, and using computers. They also enjoy travel, dancing, golfing, and hiking, woodworking, beach life, fly fishing, motorcycles, auto racing, antique cars, and exploring new areas. Don't forget wine tasting and any sport you can imagine. Nudist and clothing-optional vacation spots are also becoming popular, or so they say. Yes, I have truly read these posts on my senior dating site.

Gardening ranks up there, but it can just mean they still mow the lawn. A few good souls do volunteer work, but the sign of the times in my California town seems to be that they volunteer to play eighteen holes of golf.

You need to fit into each other's lifestyle. If you don't golf or play tennis, in most cases it's useless to respond to men interested in those sports, because they want a companion on the course or on the court.

Some men are flexible about their hobbies and lifestyles, though not in attractive way. One bragged he had separate golfing ladies and dinner ladies, and he wanted me to be his "lunch lady." I said sweetly, "No thank you!" I don't need to be anyone's lunch lady, but if you are willing to settle for just lunch, be sure and take him up on his offer. I chose to cross him off *my* list.

Men want their own space, especially if they have been unattached a long while and are accustomed to their single lifestyle. They love their freedom to golf, travel, and do as they please; there's little time left over for dating, which leaves you in the position of trying to fit into their schedule. If the man is worth it, give that relationship a try, but make *sure* you find a comfortable spot in his life. Don't ever settle for feeling like an afterthought.

Age is a surprisingly important issue with men. Somewhere in the male instruction manual, it must state, "Thou shalt never be over sixty-nine years of age," no matter what age is printed on their driver's license.

I don't know why we think we have license to lie about our age if we're hiding behind a computer screen. *We are who we are*; so, ladies and gentlemen, get real and be honest. I don't know how to get across to people that age is truly only a number. If you're afraid to tell your real age, remember that with luck you'll be face-to-face with the person you lied to.

When you write to someone and don't get a response, he may think you're too old for his liking. Many men want much younger women; some need a younger woman to turn them on, or at least they think they do.

Not everyone checks their email every day, so often it takes a week or so to get a response. I've sent follow-up emails to men I was interested in, and yes, often they did respond to my second attempt.

Many men feel they only need to post a photo on any given dating site, sit back, and wait for their mailbox to fill up. Unfortunately, that's probably true, considering the ratio of available men to women.

No false advertising, please!

If I could speak to a roomful of men, I would explain these few but important dating facts of life:

- *Timing*: Please arrive at least five to ten minutes early for your date; welcome her outside the restaurant if possible. A woman feels awkward and self-conscious when she walks into a restaurant on your first date looking for you.
- *Attitude*. Don't make a woman feel you are doing her a favor by just showing up!

Boys and Their Toys, and the Games They Play

- *Muscle flexing.* Take a minute and stand naked in front of a mirror to see what we ladies see. Too many men post a photo with their muscles flexed and shirt open like they're Mr. Universe.
- *Clothing.* It wouldn't hurt most gentlemen to tuck a shirt into a pair of nice walking shorts, jeans, or slacks, perhaps even put on a belt. I am sure most of you own a pair of loafers or nice tennis shoes.
- *Photos.* Women tell me a profile shot of a bare chest or shirt open to the waist means the man is advertising his virility and looking for a hot woman and a one-night stand. Now, if that's what you want (and that's the case for many seniors of both sexes), show your manly chest; those ladies lucky enough to land on your profile will know what you're offering. Just remember, if you can't get it up, no false advertising, *please.*
- *Hair.* When a man wears a baseball cap in his profile photo, I wonder: Does he *really* think I won't notice there's no hair under his hat if we meet? Bald is beautiful, gentlemen; take off your hats and show us your true selves. Most women don't mind a man being bald—but that doesn't mean the man should grow

a beard and mustache to compensate. Facial hair doesn't appeal to all women.
- *Grooming.* Most important (and non-negotiable) is a man's grooming. I feel *all* men need to be well groomed, especially if they hope to appeal to a lovely lady, and dressed in clean, unstained, and unwrinkled clothes. A dab of the right cologne is always a plus.

Outdoorsmen and golfers are weathered from years in the sun with dry, flaky skin, and they need to investigate skin lotion at this stage of their lives, especially on their arms; it will make a world of difference.

Men don't realize how quickly their skin gives away their age. When a man's face is deeply wrinkled yet he says he is sixty-five, well, hello! Women can tell in a heartbeat if he's probably pushing seventy-five.

Most men would benefit from a pedicure and manicure. I always smile when a big, brawny man walks bravely into the nail salon. The more confident the man, the more he will take notice of the things you prefer.

Their sexual games

I was delighted to meet one eighty-year-old date.

Boys and Their Toys, and the Games They Play

Laurence and I had a great deal in common from our active business lives, and he considered himself a very trendy Los Angeles man about town. He took me to elegant restaurants, we drank fine wines, and he loved to show off his favorite Ferrari of the day (yes, he had three).

When we first met, I felt all Laurence wanted was a lovely lady on his arm, but then he began to brag about his sexual performance. Still being a bit naïve, I thought he was just kidding, considering he was over eighty. He kept up the sexual comments, and I realized he was serious.

When Laurence boasted about a pole he had installed in his bedroom, and I finally figured out that he wanted me to use the pole in erotic ways, I couldn't get away fast enough. Now, I like sex as much as the next person, but he was just a dirty old man. I was not about to become a notch on his bedpost, or on his pole, for that matter.

Too many men remain fixated on their sex lives from their younger days, rather than adjusting to their more modest sex drive and ability at sixty-five and beyond. These men need to get past the "I am my penis" theory, which may or may not serve them well as a senior.

There are better ways than bragging about virility and toys to set the stage for seduction and sex.

Anticipation can be a powerful aphrodisiac. Teasing phone calls that imply your intent or his can get the mind working hours or days in advance, priming the pump, so to say.

> *Men are like fine wine—some turn to vinegar, but the best improve with age.*
> —**Pope John XXIII**

Many men don't initiate sex because they fear the inability to get erections and perform, and that one issue can lead to their avoiding sex altogether.

What about no sex?

There's nothing wrong with platonic relationships. If his expectations match yours, a platonic connection can be a wonderful thing. Sometimes men do only want the company of a woman, not a sexual relationship. Some want affection and support—a hand to hold and help in emotional matters. It's wonderful to have a good friend, and the right man can be a great addition to your life.

If a woman has been damaged by a terrible marriage, a friendly ear and companionship may be just what you need. A platonic male friend can offer the wonderful gift of his presence, and you can welcome his emotional and physical comfort.

11

IT'S NOT ALL ABOUT *YOU*

The big secret is that there is no big secret.
—**Oprah Winfrey**

After my experience with the Cowboy, I found myself back on the internet. Somehow, I still thought that finding a man was a game, and I was playing by the rules. I was *so* wrong.

I was trying to recapture my life with my husband with each new man I dated, and my constant comparisons left them (and me) on the outside looking in. It took me far too long to realize that I'd rejected many wonderful men who might have been spectacular boyfriends. I was too wrapped up in my old dreams and desires to appreciate many of the new men who appreciated me.

While I thought I was trying to fit into their

world, I was always asking them to fit into *mine*, just as I had done with the Cowboy. My dates weren't as assertive as my strong husband had been. *I* was the one making the decisions. *I* chose the activities, whether it was the place I wanted to dine, the movie I wanted to see, or the trip I wanted to take.

I should have encouraged my dates to take the lead and suggest what we were going to do. I should have been more eager to find out what they wanted to do. Instead, it was all about *me*. Men went along with my suggestions, then just went along, and then they were gone.

It took me far too long to learn (the hard way) that dating is a balance and you must compromise. Your dates may not be perfect, but when you take time to learn the qualities they possess, that not-so-perfect man can become suddenly very appealing.

When I finally realized what I was doing, my focus changed; writing this book became my mission.

I gathered a great deal of information from study groups, and I spent hours on the telephone with many long-time friends and acquaintances. Everyone who dated had an opinion, and they all were eager to share their great stories.

It was a shock to learn why we seniors *truly* date. Our motives for dating are simple, and they boil down to two key needs: a *dinner companion* and *sex partner*.

This bit of insight doesn't say much for our good dating intentions, does it?

Online dating has become a popular topic on many morning television talk shows and often makes the evening news. Too many times, the media only report the negative side of internet dating by giving sad statistics. They sensationalize the senior scams and don't mention the wonderful connections the internet brings to people of every age all over the world.

I still can't figure out what my future will be, but I want to spend it dancing in high heels and having great sex with a wonderful man. I just need to keep searching. I had the right man for fifty-one years, so, until a new Mr. Right comes along, I will continue my quest. Hopefully, an amazing man will pop up on my computer dating site tomorrow.

Conclusion

Life is short and it's here to be lived.
—**Kate Winslet, Actress**

Friends who lived vicariously through my wild days and nights with the Cowboy and my many other dates thought I had the best senior soap opera going. Since they knew my love of writing, they all encouraged me to write this book.

When I re-read their emails now, I smile at the truth they were trying to show me. Sometimes it's best to listen to your friends, especially those who have known you most of your life. Will you heed their advice? Probably not. Often you must go it alone, follow your heart and hope the right person will come along for you to love.

Romance is a gift. Finding a partner at any age

who will offer companionship and love is your goal, and to achieve it, you must stay in the game, and that game may be a computer dating service.

Is it worth the effort? *Of course* it is. It is time consuming, and you may suffer from email fatigue, but dating at our age is like target practice. Eventually you will hit a bull's eye.

If we're still healthy at sixty-plus, we will probably enjoy a happy and productive life for years. Fulfilling sexual activity can be a wonderful extra benefit to our retirement years. As a mature adult, you can be less inhibited, more open, and more romantic than you were when you were young.

First you must allow yourself the freedom to admit someone new into your life.

You may not find your perfect match on the first date. It may take many dates, but if the thought of quitting ever enters your mind, re-read this book. Finding your ideal new person is very possible, and it's up to you.

I hope I've encouraged you to make some positive changes for your future. We have the choice to decide what we want to make of our remaining years, and we have the time to enjoy new friends.

Life for many of us has taken a new turn and we've traveled down a road we didn't expect. My

Conclusion

mission is to bring help to people all over the world by changing the way we perceive ourselves, and by helping you understand our brave new world of internet dating.

Whether you are retired domestic engineers, teachers, business people, or entrepreneurs, whether you were divorced, widowed, or never married, it's now *your* time to shine.

Don't miss the opportunity to meet the person of your dreams. Romantic love can find you at any age—you're *never* too old. Reach out to anyone who appeals to you and learn from the experiences of each new date. Don't just sit and complain that there are no good men or women out there. Dating is about trying different matches until you find the one that fits happily and comfortably into your life as it is today.

You have earned the right to search for the person of your dreams, so don't just sit there! Climb into the boat with the rest of us, put your oar in the water, row side-by-side with us, and move your life along. What's waiting for you on the other side may be a wonderful person with open arms, and then you'll truly know what you're doing the rest of your life.

Good luck to each of you! Happy rowing.

Appendix

Stay Healthy and Safe

*Love is something from Heaven
to worry the hell out of us.*
—**Dolly Parton**

*W*hat I am about to tell you about staying healthy and safe is not meant to replace medical advice. I am not an expert by any means, and I encourage you to research on your own, talk to your doctor, and be tested.

A half-century of monogamy had blissfully kept me in the dark about sexually transmitted diseases. Since I was writing this book and had to become more knowledgeable, I turned to my doctor. These days, responsible doctors tell you, "When you sleep with someone, you sleep with every person he or she ever slept with." My doctor did more; she gave me pamphlets to read, and she sent me to the Center for Disease Control, the CDC, for more research.

I called the CDC and asked my questions of a millennial employee on the other end of the line; I don't think she believed me when I told her I needed research for a book I was writing.

A week later, a large stuffed yellow manila envelope with CDC stamped all over it filled my mailbox, and the material was truly enlightening. When I understood the possible consequence of unsafe sex, I was astonished and horrified.

If you practice safe sex, which means being willing to be screened for STDs, having an honest dialogue with your prospective partner, and using a condom, you should be able to have a wonderful, infection-free sex life.

I cannot stress enough the importance of being screened for STDs, both you and your partner; it's the first stage of safe sex. Most of these diseases and infections are not obvious, and the only way you might know you have them is to be tested. If you have a STD, do *not* have sex while you are being treated.

If there are sores on areas not covered by the condom, infection is still possible. If you're not sure of your partner's health, it may mean resorting to mutual masturbation, rather than having conventional intercourse.

Syphilis is a dangerous STD, one that can be virtually invisible. Often patients don't know they have syphilis because rash, fever, sore throat, joint pain and other symptoms may mask the disease. A syphilitic sore, called a chancre, appears at the location of the original infection (usually mouth, vagina, or anus), and contact with the chancre is contagious. After the chancre goes away, there may be secondary symptoms such as a rash.

The disease stays in your body if not treated. While most people go into a latent, or inactive, stage, syphilis can cause dementia, insanity, organ failure, and blindness. Fortunately, syphilis is curable with antibiotics.

Gonorrhea, also known as the clap, is a far more common STD, and about half a million people catch it per year. *It's important that you know this:* Reported cases of gonorrhea in adults 65 and over increased by *90%* between 2010 and 2014. Gonorrhea can be cured with by antibiotics, though harder-to-treat antibiotic-resistant varieties are becoming widespread. Always using condoms is the best way to protect yourself from infection.

Symptoms vary depending on which part of

your body is affected, but they usually include pain and some oozing. If untreated, gonorrhea can cause some serious health issues, including pelvic inflammatory disease, an infection that happens if the disease spreads inside your body.

There is no cure for genital herpes; fortunately, it does not usually cause serious health problems. It's a common viral disease among sexually active men and women; one in five adults have the virus, and only ten percent know that they have it. Even those without active symptoms can infect their partner.

Painful blisters or pimple-like sores and flu-like feelings are the most common symptoms, and they usually show up within two weeks of exposure. Genital herpes is treated with anti-viral medicines, and it's best to start treatment as soon as possible.

Condoms can reduce your risk. Remember, a condom only protects the area of the body it covers; exposed areas can become infected. When sores come back, you're having an "outbreak" and are very contagious.

My doctor pointed out hepatitis as another sexually transmitted disease. If you're sexually active, the Hepatitis A and B vaccine may be recommended for you. (There is no vaccine for Hepatitis C, but fortunately it's not spread by

Stay Healthy and Safe

sexual contact.) Any version of hepatitis is of special concern to diabetics; it means inflammation of the liver, and it can cause temporary or permanent liver damage.

It may surprise you to learn that an estimated 1.2 million people are living with HIV in the United States. Of those who are affected, approximately 156,300 don't know they have the disease, because they might not have symptoms for years. Due to ignorance and lack of testing, 13% of the people who have HIV don't know to protect a partner from catching the virus, and they also don't know how to keep themselves from developing full-blown AIDS.

Although there is no cure, people with HIV can live long, healthy lives today thanks to early detection and the new more effective treatments.

HPV (human papillomavirus) has been in the news with much talk of HPV vaccinations for teenagers before they become sexually active. The HPV virus can lead to cancer of the cervix, vagina, throat, and anus. (Did you know that cervical cancer is now considered a STD? True, and a surprise to most of us.)

Another variety of HPV causes genital warts, which don't cause cancer.

Other STDs include chlamydia and bacterial

vaginosis. They won't kill you, but you'll certainly wish you'd been more careful.

No one should be embarrassed or afraid to talk to their doctor about such serious issues or be embarrassed to ask a partner to produce proof of negative tests. Anyone with an STD should *always* disclose their situation to a potential partner before having sex.

The bottom line is *you must get tested*. We must become responsible, smart sexual partners.

Unfortunately, statistics show most people don't know they have an STD or are contagious. If they've been sexually active with multiple partners and don't usually use protection, the odds are they've been exposed. If you have unprotected sex with them, you've been exposed, too!

About the Author

Carol Thomas is a Midwest girl raised with old-fashioned Midwest values, someone who never dreamed she'd be sharing the intimate secrets of online dating with thousands of strangers.

When she moved to Arizona to attend college, she met and married a John Wayne look-alike who cherished her for more than fifty years.

Carol's writing career began as the society editor of a small-town newspaper in Orange County, California. She also volunteered with local civic organizations, teaching them the basics of publicity and public relations. Carol became the first woman accepted by the local Toastmasters club, at that time a male-only organization.

When Carol's family business triggered a move to the Palm Springs area, she showed her entrepreneurial streak through owning her own retail business for the next twenty-five years. She continued her love of writing by serving on the executive board of directors of her local business association for many years, promoting its many member businesses. Her published articles appeared in numerous trade magazines.

She was the consummate family social director, raised three children and was a happily married grandmother when the unthinkable happened and her life forever changed.

A few years following her husband's death she made the decision to reach out and find happiness through online dating. Carol's experiences, both good *and* bad, led to her decision to write this book in hopes of helping other struggling with new beginnings. She firmly believes it's "NEVER TOO LATE" to find a new relationship.

Dedication

This book is dedicated to my remarkable husband, who loved and cherished me for more than 50 years. I lost him far too soon.

Life goes on in ways we never anticipate, and he would be the first to wish me success in all I attempt, whether it's finding a second love or becoming an author.

I will succeed for him.

*Memory is the diary
that we all carry about with us.*
— **Oscar Wilde**

www.ingramcontent.com/pod-product-compliance
Lightning Source LLC
Chambersburg PA
CBHW032358040426
42451CB00006B/56